The True Me

How I Became a National Risk in Sweden

Adam Youssef

Into Action

The Guy in Blue

"We have evacuated the area, and he's surrounded. I have a clear shot and I'm ready for your orders, over," Officer Anna replied to Sergeant Eric, her voice steady despite the tension crackling through the radio.
"Stay alert. He's got a bomb belt on him. If he tries to stand up, shoot him, over," Sergeant Eric commanded, his tone firm and unyielding.
"Roger that. Out," Anna responded, her eyes narrowing as she focused on the figure lying on the ground.

Now, let's zoom in a little: there is a guy in blue, lying face down on the cold, wet ground. His hands are cuffed behind his back, rain trickling down its surface. He's thinking, "I'm bored, it's been several hours like this. Should I turn to the other side to see who's shouting at me? Should I stand up to scare them a little?"

That's me in the blue. And this is how it all began.

✳   ✳   ✳

As we Begin

The Struggle to be Fair

Let me begin by outlining the purpose of this book—a journey aimed at fostering a crucial trait within myself and others: the ability to approach individuals without hasty judgement, yet without ignoring that aspect entirely. It's about fairness.

This is particularly important for those who have read about my crime, formed an impression, and spread hate and threats. I'm not saying that I don't deserve the consequences of my actions or that such actions are normal and should be ignored.

Instant judgement and total disregard are both extremes to be avoided. And that's why this trait is a precious trait, it is the struggle to be fair.

Reflecting on the words of Prophet Muhammad (peace be upon him), who stated that all sons of Adam are fallible.

Our mistakes vary in magnitude—some may be as severe as murder, while others as minor as an unfair comment on a post. The only way to respond to our mistakes is to repent and do good to offset the bad.

Recognizing the impact of my past actions, I found writing this book to be the most effective way to reach a broad audience and impart positive values, contrasting the negativity I once spread.

This journey begins at the very inception of my memories, highlighting pivotal events that moulded my radical mindset.

*　　*　　*

Childhood Innocence

Finding Joy in the Quiet

One of my earliest childhood memories takes me back to a serene night when my parents were away at the hospital, eagerly anticipating the arrival of my baby brother, Dyaa. At the time, I was just three years old, and my older sister Sarah, who was seven, was my only companion at home.

The atmosphere in our house was draped in tranquil stillness that night, as if the very air had settled into a comforting embrace. The silence was interrupted only by the soft rustling of coloured papers I held in my small hands.

I recall vividly the bright hues of those papers, their textures familiar against my fingertips, and the simple joy they brought me in that moment of anticipation. Despite my tender age, these memories remain deeply etched in my mind.

Bonding with Mom Through Song

My relationship with my mother was a tapestry woven with countless cherished moments. On ordinary days, as she bustled in the kitchen preparing meals, I would often find myself in the bedroom, my young voice filling the air with a song. When I stumbled over lyrics, I'd dash to her side, and with infinite patience, she would help me recall the words before I raced back to continue my singing.

Childhood Joy in Simple Gifts

One of my fondest memories that filled me with pure joy was when my mother returned from a trip and brought me some small plastic tea spoons and tiny sugar bags. These little treasures were quite uncommon at the time, and I was over the moon with excitement at the sight of them.

I remember clutching them with delight, my heart brimming with happiness. Each time my mother went out after that, I eagerly asked her to bring me more.

Heartbreak and Healing

There were also moments of profound disappointment and comfort. I remember a day when my father returned home without the biscuits he had promised me. Overwhelmed with disappointment, I retreated to the kitchen, tears streaming down my face. My mother attempted to console me, offering money to buy them myself, yet my sorrow held firm.

Sneaky Escapades and Mom's Surprise

On another occasion, an afternoon when I had school later in the day, my mother was busy cleaning the house. She went up to the roof to hang the freshly washed carpet so it could dry.

Knowing that my dad had hidden the Atari in the bedroom closet, I seized the opportunity.

I sneaked into the bedroom, stood on the bed, and carefully retrieved the Atari. My heart raced with excitement as I quickly connected it to the TV, eager to play. Just as I was getting started, my mother returned and discovered what I had done. Her face showed a mix of surprise and frustration, clearly not pleased with my mischievous act.

Friday Fun

Then there was one particular Friday, a day off from kindergarten, though I didn't realise it at the time. Sensing a chance for playful deception, my mother struck a bargain: finish my entire sandwich, and I could skip kindergarten. Eager to avoid it, I gladly devoured the sandwich. True to her word, she then revealed the real surprise: my cousins had set up a children's pool on the roof, awaiting my arrival.

Racing upstairs, I was greeted by the delightful sight of my cousins splashing and laughing joyfully. Our building, home to five apartments housing us, my grandpa, and three uncles, felt like a bustling community brimming with family and love.

The Royal Cup

My father used to tell me that whenever I asked for water, I would only accept it if my mother brought me the cup. No one else could fulfil this simple request for me. He used to joke, saying it was as if I were a king, afraid someone might poison me if the water came from anyone but her.

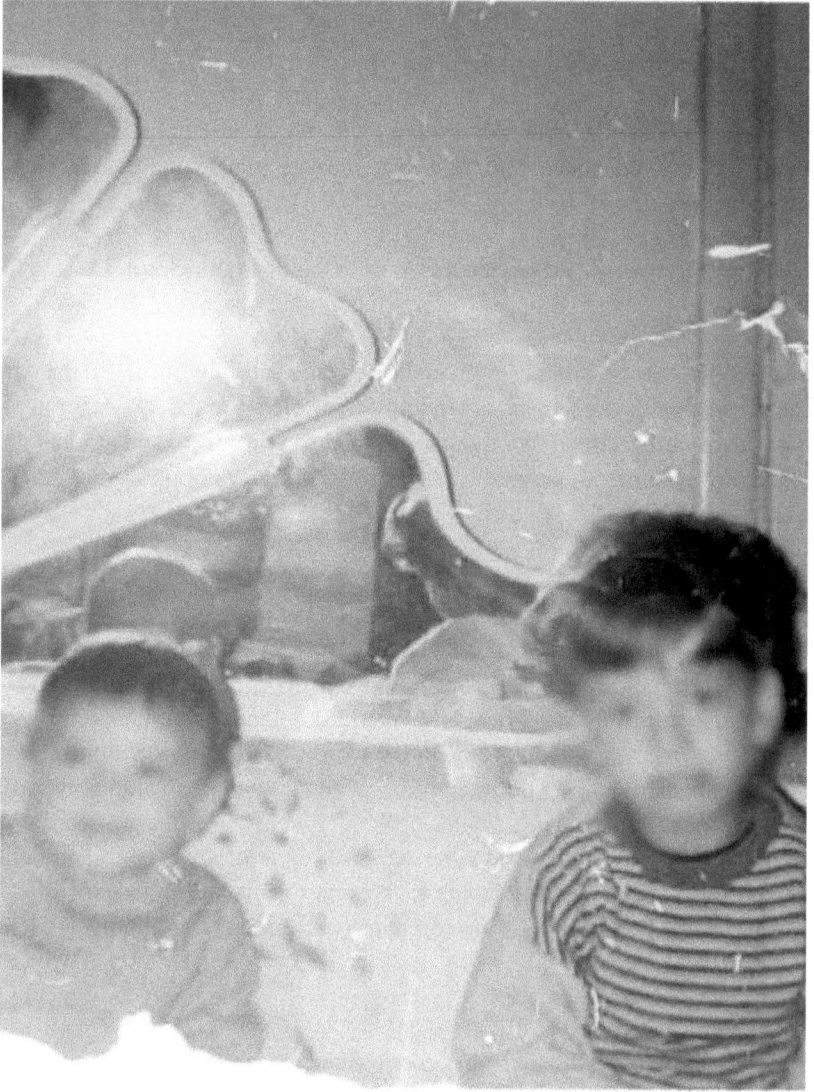

(Dyaa and I)

Silent Pain

I remember a day when we were sitting together, enjoying some fruit. As I glanced at my mother, I noticed something unusual—her eyes closed tightly, her lips pressed together, her face contorted with pain. It was a sight I had never seen before, and concern flooded my young mind.

I stared at her, worry evident on my face. Sensing my unease, she quickly offered a reassuring smile and casually mentioned that the apple was causing her discomfort.

Little did I know then, the truth behind her strained expression. It wasn't the apple that caused her pain, but rather the silent struggle of cancer she was enduring.

The Day My World Shattered

I don't remember much about her after that; I was just six years old. I spent my days at my aunt's house, where I played endlessly with my cousins, our laughter echoing through the rooms.

Then, one ordinary day, the phone rang, piercing through the cheerful noise. My aunt's face turned pale as she answered. In an instant, the room fell silent except for her choked sobs.

With trembling hands, she dropped the receiver. I stood frozen, sensing the weight of something dreadful unfolding. I knew without being told. My mother was gone.

My tears flowed uncontrollably, an overwhelming rush of sorrow, the woman whose laughter had echoed through our home, whose gentle touch had comforted me, was now a memory, lost to an invisible force that even my young mind struggled to grasp.

My Last Moments with Mom

The next thing I remember, we were in a pick-up truck—my father, Dyaa, and I—surrounded by an unbearable silence, accompanied only by the presence of my mother's lifeless body. I watched as my father, with solemn grace, uncovered her face. He gently urged us to say our goodbyes.

Dyaa summoned his courage and leaned in to kiss her farewell. But for me, a mixture of shyness and profound grief held me back. I stood there, aching to touch her one last time, but unable to overcome the overwhelming sense of loss.

My World Shifted

From that day forward, my world shifted. Childhood innocence shattered. The colours seemed muted, the once-familiar surroundings now strange and unfamiliar. The absence of her presence was a void I couldn't fill, and the ache of her absence became a silent burden I carried with me.

Burying My Mother

When we arrived at the village in Daraa, the birthplace of both my grandfathers, it was to lay my mother to rest. The memory of the burial remains vivid: a large pit dug into the earth, and within it, a smaller one where they gently placed my mother.

The night enveloped us, the darkness echoing with murmurs of mourning and illuminated by the soft glow of lanterns. It was a scene etched deeply into my memory, a stark tableau of loss and finality witnessed through the innocent eyes of a six-year-old.

Family Moments Post-Burial

After the burial, we returned to the house where my mother's uncle and many relatives lived. We gathered outside near the main door, and four of my distant cousins, all sisters, surrounded me with curious eyes.

They gently urged me to describe the burial, their questions filled with a mixture of innocence and concern. I did my best to recount the sombre details, still struggling to comprehend the stark reality of the situation myself.

Healing Through Love

These four cousins brought immense joy into my life. Each spring, I eagerly awaited our visits to their home, where they showered me with love and treated me like a treasured guest. Their affection became a soothing balm for my young heart, especially in the wake of my mother's passing.

I remember one particular day when they playfully asked me, "Who do you like the most?" Without hesitation, I pointed to Wisam, and her delighted response was to burst into a joyful dance, revelling in being my favourite. These moments, brimming with laughter and love, remain among my happiest childhood memories.

A Warm Haven

In the village, my relatives always greeted me with kindness and patience, never chastising me for the mischief typical of a child.

Their warmth enveloped me, creating a sense of safety and unconditional love that helped me navigate the difficult days after losing my mother.

Springtime Bliss

The village itself appeared as a paradise through my young eyes, especially during the springtime. I have vivid memories of running and playing in fields ablaze with flowers of every hue imaginable. It was like stepping into a scene from a storybook—a serene heaven where I felt utterly free and joyous.

* * *

Unexpected Turn

Anticipating the Unknown

About eight months after my mother passed away, my father took on the challenge of fulfilling both parental roles for my two siblings and me. During this period, he began discussing the prospect of marrying someone new.

The idea of a stranger entering our lives felt unsettling and unfamiliar. My cousin, perhaps sensing my unease, playfully teased that she would be an old lady, which only added to my apprehension. However, as it turned out—spoiler alert—she wasn't.

A New Beginning

A few months later, we travelled to my stepmother's village for their wedding. Alongside my father, sister, and four-year-old brother, I felt a mix of anticipation and unease.

After the ceremony, we returned home with her. That first night, she was incredibly kind, laughing and playing with us. I felt a wave of happiness and relief, thinking that everything would be alright.

When Warmth Turns to Hostility

However, as time passed, her demeanour shifted. She grew increasingly irritable, strict, and unpredictable in mood. The woman who had initially appeared so gentle had transformed, and life at home gradually became tumultuous for me, Sarah and Dyaa.The love and warmth that once defined our household gave way to palpable tension and hostility.

Finding Solace Amidst Tension

Yet amidst the turmoil, there were fleeting moments of relief—brief respites when she travelled to visit her own family and stayed away for a few days.

I remember waking up on those mornings, realising she wasn't home, and celebrating with my sister and brother. Those days provided a rare break from the constant stress and fear that had become our daily companions.

A Father Absorbed

My father, engrossed in his work, often seemed oblivious to the tumult brewing at home. I remember instances when we gathered the courage to voice our concerns about her behaviour, and he would express frustration with her. However, his attention was often fleeting, absorbed once more by the demands of his profession.

Effects of Family Conflict

The daily struggles and clashes with my stepmother cast a long shadow over my upbringing. Her mood swings and strict demeanour created an unpredictable environment fraught with tension. Despite my father's intermittent interventions, his absence from our day-to-day interactions left me feeling adrift in a sea of familial discord.

Confronting Conflict

The turbulent atmosphere persisted until I reached around 15 years old. By then, I had grown resilient enough to defy her authority with impunity. As I asserted my independence, the household dynamic underwent a gradual shift. Yet, the wounds inflicted during those formative years remained etched in my memory.

The Guy in Blue

Hmm, let's go back a little, I'm looking at a bookshop, it's the only thing I can look at, its interior dark and foreboding. The night enveloped me in its inky blackness, amplifying my isolation. Where has everyone gone? Just moments ago, a crowd surrounded me, their words filling the air. Now, I was utterly alone. Would I die here tonight?

My mind began to race, flashing back to memories of my life. Each detail, every laugh, and every cry played before my eyes like a film reel. I saw my family, my father's calming voice echoing in my ears. And my mother—her love, I felt a desperate plea rising from deep within my soul, crying out for help, but no one could hear it.

*   *   *

Childhood Bonds

At School

At school, I was the shy kid who always stuck close to his older cousin, Ammar. Despite technically being my uncle, he was only three months older, and we shared the same class for what felt like an eternity. Ammar was way more outgoing than me. We consistently achieved top marks, but he was naturally smarter than me. The only subject where I surpassed him was English.

A Heartfelt Gesture

One memory from fourth grade stands out vividly in my mind. Ammar claimed the top spot in our class, with me following closely behind in second place. Both of us earned excellent grades, but it was Ammar who received gifts from the teacher to celebrate his achievement—sunglasses and a toy. Despite our close bond, the moment stung.

As he opened his gifts, I felt a lump in my throat and tears welling up. Trying to hide my emotions, I excused myself and retreated to the stairwell. There, I let myself cry uncontrollably, the weight of my disappointment was too much to bear silently.

Ammar must have heard me, because he soon found me and tried to console me. "Didn't you know these gifts are for both of us?" he said gently, his voice filled with kindness. I knew he was trying to lift my spirits, and I appreciated the gesture deeply. Still unable to shake off my feelings of inadequacy, I replied, "It's alright, you can keep them."

The gesture spoke volumes about his character and the bond we shared, even in moments of personal pain and silent rivalry.

Crafting Memories

Dyaa, Ammar, our uncle's son Salem, and I were inseparable. As children close in age, we were always inventing new games to play. Our creativity knew no bounds; sometimes we crafted intricate toys out of wood, other times we worked with paper. We often made small cars complete with tiny engines, batteries, and lights, spending countless hours perfecting our creations and enjoying the fruits of our labour. Our shared adventures and inventive play were the foundation of our unbreakable bond.

Curiosity Unleashed

Our curiosity and creativity were sparked by anything exciting we read in school books or student magazines. I remember vividly when we learned about helium and its ability to lift balloons. Enthralled by the concept, we embarked on a mission to create our first flying car. Without proper tools or internet access for research, our attempt was hilariously doomed to failure.

The Magic of Childhood

Digimon Adventure was the cornerstone of our childhood, it fueled our imaginations and shaped our adventures.

The first satellite dish was at my grandfather's house, so my brother and I would eagerly wake up at 6 AM, head to Ammar's place, and watch two episodes of Digimon Adventure before the day began.

Harry Potter inspired us to craft our own wizard wands, complete with lights. We memorised countless spells and duelled each other in magical battles.

Our Yu-Gi-Oh! tournaments were legendary. We would gather in the living room, the floor strewn with cards, and dive into intense duels.

Pokémon was another major influence on us. We were so captivated by the series that we invented our own Pokémon game with unique rules. Armed with paper and markers, we crafted our own cards and engaged in epic duels, our imaginations transforming our living room into a vibrant battlefield filled with our custom-created Pokémon.

These series were more than just shows to us; they were the fabric of our childhood, weaving together countless hours of shared joy, creativity, and friendship.

Under the Stars

Our aunt's home was a frequent destination for my siblings and me. They often visited us too, fostering a close bond between our families.

Nestled near a mountain, their place offered a stunning cliffside view, which became a popular nighttime gathering spot. It was there, under the vast starlit sky, that I experienced my first taste of young love.

Innocence and Awkwardness

As a shy boy, initiating conversations was a daunting task, so I relied on charming looks and timid smiles. There was a girl who often exchanged glances with me, creating a silent but palpable connection. I confided in Dyaa and cousin Mohammad about her, and they noticed our mutual interest. Together, we concocted a plan to give her the phone number of Mohammad's sister—an elaborate scheme, considering our lack of easy access to phones at that age.

Instead of simply approaching her, we decided on a more intricate strategy. Aware that our time was limited, we hurried to a nearby supermarket to borrow a pen and paper. With nervous hands, we hastily scribbled down the number. The hardest part remained: how to deliver it to her discreetly.

My courage finally surfaced as we sat in the car, about to depart. As the engine started, I stole one last glance at her and impulsively tossed the paper in her direction, hoping she would notice and call the number.

Looking back, it was a clumsy yet endearing attempt at romance—a testament to the innocence and awkwardness of childhood crushes, where even the smallest gestures carried immense significance.

Transforming from Shy to Shine

By the time I reached 10th grade and turned 16, I started shedding my shy demeanour and embracing a more outgoing persona. It was a conscious effort to push myself beyond my comfort zone.

By 11th grade, I began to feel like the most popular guy in school—a transformation that seemed almost surreal. Suddenly, people knew me even if I didn't know them.

I worked hard to cultivate a sense of confidence and charm that attracted attention. Whether it was participating in school events, making new friends, or simply being more sociable, I found myself at the centre of school life. The once quiet and reserved kid was now enjoying the limelight and relishing in the newfound popularity.

Chasing Thrills

However, embracing my newfound social life came with unintended consequences. As I became more involved in school social circles, my academic performance started to decline. No longer was I achieving the top marks I once effortlessly attained. Instead of prioritising my studies, I found myself immersed in pranks on teachers and skipping school every Tuesday to rendezvous with my girlfriend in a public park.

* * *

The Unseen Uprising

From Stability to Struggle

Around that time, the unexpected uprising in Syria began—an event that took everyone by surprise, considering the country's strict laws and the pervasive fear of the regime. Syria had long been perceived as stable under authoritarian rule, with dissent and opposition largely suppressed.

However, against all odds, a wave of protests and demonstrations erupted, challenging the entrenched regime and its grip on power. What started as isolated incidents soon escalated into a nationwide movement, fueled by discontent, grievances, and a desire for change among the Syrian people.

The uprising marked a significant turning point in the region's political landscape, defying earlier assumptions and reshaping global perceptions of Syria. It was a stark reminder of the unpredictable nature of political unrest and the resilience of people in demanding their rights and freedoms, even in the face of severe repression.

Origins of Conflict

The unrest began in Daraa, my family's hometown. My ID clearly indicated my Daraa origin, which complicated matters at checkpoints, where scrutiny was heightened for anyone from Daraa.

The conflict in Daraa ignited in March 2011, when a group of teenagers was arrested for anti-government graffiti. Their harsh treatment and detention sparked outrage among the local population. Protests erupted, demanding their release and calling for greater political freedoms. The government's brutal crackdown on these demonstrations further fueled the dissent, transforming the local unrest into a broader national uprising. As the conflict spread, the situation deteriorated with alarming speed, affecting even previously safe cities like Damascus.

The Symphony of War

I vividly remember the day the conflict reached our neighbourhood in Damascus. It began with the power going out, plunging us into an eerie, oppressive darkness that lasted for days. The distant sound of bombings grew steadily louder, until they seemed to be right on our doorstep. The air was filled with the cacophony of weapon clashes, the deafening blasts of mortar shells, the menacing hum of helicopters overhead, and the relentless roar of warfare. The once familiar sounds of daily life were replaced by the terrifying symphony of conflict, creating a new, harrowing reality that enveloped us completely.

(A Scene of Destruction in Syria)

In the Heat of Despair

That summer was unbearably hot, the oppressive heat exacerbated by relentless power outages and shuttered shops. My three years old cute little sister. We placed her in a big bucket of water to cool her down, a makeshift remedy that broke my heart. Seeing her tiny, vulnerable body in that bucket brought tears to my eyes. My anger boiled over, directed at the Shabiha, the regime's ruthless enforcers, who I blamed for our misery. In that moment, a fierce determination ignited within me. I resolved to join the Free Army, driven by a desperate need to protect my family and fight back against the forces that had torn our lives apart.

A Silent Farewell

The next morning, my father asked me to buy some food for breakfast. I wandered the eerily quiet streets until I found an open falafel shop. The aroma of freshly fried falafel filled the air, momentarily lifting the oppressive weight of the conflict. I bought the food and headed back home, my mind swirling with the decision I had made.

When I reached our doorstep, I paused, taking a deep breath. Instead of going inside, I gently placed the bag of food at the door. The sunlight cast long shadows as I turned away, my heart pounding with a mix of fear and determination. Without saying a word to anyone about my plan, I walked away.

An Uncertain Journey

I walked to the main road, my steps heavy with uncertainty, and waited for a bus. My mind raced with questions, each more daunting than the last. How would I find the Free Army? What would I say to them? What could I possibly do next? My plan, if it could be called that, was driven purely by raw emotion, a desperate leap into the unknown with no clear direction or certainty.

Desolate Streets

When I arrived in the town, it felt like stepping into a ghost town. The streets were eerily empty, and an unsettling silence hung in the air. As I wandered through the silent, crumbling buildings, a profound sadness washed over me. I knew my family would soon start wondering where I was, and the thought of their worry tugged at my heart, deepening the loneliness of my journey.

A Stranger's Warning

Eventually, I spotted a man in the distance. He seemed concerned, his brow furrowed as he noticed a young guy like me walking alone in such a perilous place. His eyes, filled with a mix of curiosity and care, met mine as he approached.

"Where are you going?" he asked, his voice tinged with genuine concern.

"Just visiting my aunt," I replied, trying to sound casual despite the tension in the air.

"Be careful, The army is all over the place." he warned, glancing around nervously.

I nodded, offering him a reassuring smile, though my heart raced with apprehension. With a final nod, I continued on my way, his words echoing in my mind.

Under the Bridge

I reached a main road that stretched ahead, usually vibrant with the cacophony of car horns, bustling shops, and a throng of people. But that day, it lay eerily deserted.

Continuing on, my eyes caught sight of a bridge up ahead. Below it, numerous army units stood sentinel with tanks, a formidable presence that sent a chill down my spine. Fear gripped me like a vice, rendering me speechless and unsure of how to proceed. Every instinct screamed at me to flee.

I quickened my pace, desperate to evade any notice, and turned sharply into a narrow side road. Relief washed over me in a wave, but uncertainty loomed large. Now what? Would I stumble upon the Free Army by chance in some forgotten corner?

A Lifeline in Crisis

Suddenly, my phone pierced the tense silence with its shrill ringtone. Startled, I fumbled to answer it, my heart racing as I heard my sister's tearful voice on the other end. Her worried questions cut through my turmoil.

"I'll be back soon," I reassured her, trying to sound composed despite the chaos around me. The relief of hearing her voice washed over me, momentarily grounding me in the reality of my family's concern.

In that moment, a surge of conflicting emotions coursed through me. Relief flooded in as I realised I no longer needed to pursue my reckless plan. Yet, anxiety gnawed at me, knowing I still had to face my family's inevitable reaction to my abrupt disappearance.

A Pause for Reflection and Respite

I retraced my steps to the familiar Souq in Old Damascus, seeking solace in a renowned coffee shop. The contrast between the quiet streets I had just left and the lively atmosphere of the Souq was striking. Here, life carried on as usual with bustling crowds weaving through narrow alleys, the aroma of spices mingling in the air, and the melodious chatter of merchants hawking their wares.

Taking a seat, I ordered a cup of tea, the warmth soothing against my trembling hands. The familiar clink of cups and saucers, the rhythmic hum of conversations, and the comforting routine of preparing my drink helped to steady my nerves amidst the turmoil of my thoughts.

Homecoming

As I returned home, a heavy sense of anticipation hung in the air, mingling with the lingering echoes of my sudden departure. The atmosphere inside the house felt charged with emotions—relief intertwined with simmering anger, creating an uneasy tension that awaited resolution.

Entering the familiar surroundings, I braced myself to confront my father and sister. Their faces reflected a myriad of emotions—concern etched deeply into their features, yet tempered with the underlying currents of frustration and worry. The weight of their mixed feelings bore down on me as I prepared to explain myself.

In the ensuing moments, voices rose and fell in heated exchanges, emotions spilling over as we navigated the aftermath of my impulsive actions. Yet, as the intensity of the confrontation ebbed, a sense of understanding began to emerge, slowly diffusing the tension that had gripped us.

Echoes of Chaos

Later that same day, I watched in surprise as the news flashed across the screen: Jabhat al-Nusra, a faction formerly aligned with the Islamic State in Syria, had orchestrated a devastating suicide car bombing at the headquarters in Damascus. The impact of this event reverberated through the city, signifying a shift in the trajectory of the conflict.

From Shock to Routine

Weeks passed, and the echoes of war became an unsettling backdrop to daily life. The once-shocking sounds of conflict gradually melded into the fabric of everyday existence. For many, there were no viable alternatives but to persist with their routines, and our family was no exception.

Hemiplegia's Impact on Our Family

That summer, just before our third and final year in high school, our household faced a new challenge: my grandfather, Ammar's father, suffered from a hemiplegia, a condition that left him partially paralyzed. The impact was profound, particularly for Ammar and his mother, who bore the weight of caring for him in his newfound state of dependency. Every aspect of his daily life now required assistance—walking, showering, and every basic need.

Bread and Bullets

Ammar and I managed to secure a summer job at a factory that produced baguette bread for restaurants. While we worked, my younger brother often stayed home to keep our grandpa company. One morning, as we headed to work, we noticed the street was eerily empty, an unusual sight that set us on edge.

Suddenly, the sharp cracks of gunfire and the unmistakable sounds of weapon clashes erupted nearby, shattering the morning calm. Panic surged through us as we turned and ran back home, our hearts pounding in our chests. Fear gripped me, but Ammar, always the one to inject humour into tense situations, spotted a cockroach scurrying across the street.

"Cockroach!" he shouted, his voice exaggerated in mock horror, trying to lighten the moment. At the time, I couldn't bring myself to laugh, the terror too overwhelming. But looking back, that moment became a funny memory, a small beacon of light in the midst of our darkest days.

A Summer Quest for Education

Halfway through the summer, Ammar, our two friends, and I decided to search for a summer school to prepare for our crucial final year, which would determine our university prospects. We ventured into Midan, a town in Damascus that had experienced unrest before, but seemed relatively calm when we arrived.

As we wandered through the town, we found several schools, each promising a chance to shape our academic futures. We collected their brochures and contact information, feeling a sense of purpose amid the uncertainty.

With our pockets full of school cards and our minds filled with hope, we began our journey home.

Terror on an Empty Street

As we walked down a street that was usually bustling with activity, the eerie emptiness sent shivers down our spines. We passed a bus filled with Shabiha, the notorious government militia. They eyed us silently at first, their presence heavy and menacing. Hoping to avoid trouble, we turned into a smaller road, seeking a shortcut to the bus station.

Suddenly, two Shabiha members appeared at the corner, their faces hardened with suspicion. One had an AK-47 slung casually over his shoulder, while the other, clearly the leader, clutched a walkie-talkie.

His voice, low and threatening, cut through the tense air as he demanded to know what we were doing.

Nervously, we explained our search for summer schools and showed him the cards we had collected. He sneered, his eyes narrowing with distrust.

"You're here to start a protest, aren't you?" he accused, his words dripping with hostility. Our hearts pounded with fear as we swore we weren't, but the other Shabiha member ominously reloaded his gun.

The deserted road offered no refuge, and we knew these men held absolute power. They could kill us without consequence. The leader took our IDs and scrutinised them. When he saw that Ammar and I were from Daraa, his expression darkened further.

With a sudden, brutal slap, he struck us hard across the face, the sting burning our cheeks. He kicked us to the ground and threw our IDs at us with contempt.

"Go away and never come back," he snarled, his voice a mix of rage and disdain. Trembling, we scrambled to our feet, grabbed our IDs, and fled as fast as we could, our hearts heavy with fear and humiliation. We vowed never to return to that place again.

A Tank at the Gate

When school started, it felt like stepping into a ghost town. The once vibrant corridors, usually filled with the lively chatter of students, were now eerily silent. Most of the teachers had disappeared, their absence leaving a void that echoed through the empty halls. Our English teacher had been promoted to principal, a small comfort for me since he knew me well and I had excelled in his class.

This semblance of normalcy didn't last long. We managed to attend classes for only a few days before the school was closed indefinitely. On what turned out to be our last day, a tank was ominously stationed next to the school, a stark reminder of the escalating conflict around us.

Unsure of what to do, we approached our English teacher-turned-principal to seek guidance. He seemed torn, hesitating as he weighed the options.

"Go home," he finally said, then reconsidered, "No, it's okay, enter the school." After a moment's pause, he chuckled and said, "You know what, just go home." We all laughed at the confusion and indecision, a brief moment of levity, before we turned and made our way back home, leaving the tank and the school behind us.

The Guy in Blue

The sirens of the police cars now filled the area, their lights casting eerie reflections on the walls around me. Crime scene tape cordoned off my small, self-made stage, isolating me in the very scene I had orchestrated. I was both the director and the sole actor in this tragic play.

But there were no crowds cheering. Instead, the air was thick with anger and confusion. I had worked so hard to produce this moment, yet there was no appreciation, no validation. Had I missed some crucial part? Was this really the end? Maybe there was a twist yet to come.

Anything could happen. I convinced myself to wait, to just hold on a bit longer. Yes, I would wait.

*　*　*

The Unravelling

A New Refuge

During that tumultuous time, parts of Daraa were actually safer than Damascus. As our hometown became increasingly perilous and many families fled, we decided to travel to Daraa.

In Daraa, we stayed with our aunt and resumed our schooling—me, Dyaa, and Ammar.

Salem, our other cousin, had gone to Egypt two years earlier and remained there.

From City Lights to Village Shadows

Jasem, the village we relocated to, was a stark contrast to the city life we were accustomed to. The rural setting was quieter, the pace slower. We tried to make new friends, but the absence of familiar faces was disheartening.

Many people we once knew were no longer around, their lives upended by the conflict. The weight of these changes became too much for me to bear. Reflecting on it now, it's heartbreaking to see how everything changed—the place, the sense of security, everything we once knew.

Silent Resolve

Several months had passed when I made the heart-wrenching decision to slip away to Damascus alone, quietly stealing myself away without a word to anyone. Only Ammar knew of my clandestine plan, and despite his desperate attempts to dissuade me, I insisted on absolute secrecy from our father and everyone else. The weight of my choice settled heavily on my shoulders as I navigated through the quiet streets towards the bus station, every step a mixture of determination and apprehension.

Boarding the bus bound for Damascus, I found a seat by the window and gazed out, watching the familiar landscapes blur past through a haze of emotions—fear, longing, and a persistent sense of purpose driving me forward despite the dangers ahead.

In the Hot Seat

The bus journey was fraught with tension, each mile a precarious dance through checkpoints that dotted the deserted roads. In the middle of nowhere, a checkpoint—a lone outpost in the barren landscape, manned by soldiers scrutinising every passenger.

They singled me out, perhaps because I was the youngest on board. They confiscated my phone and meticulously combed through it. Anxiety gripped me as I had deleted any incriminating photos or videos, but overlooked the potentially damning WhatsApp conversation exchanged weeks ago with a friend, expressing our frustrations and anger towards the regime.

Ordered off the bus for a more thorough search, I stepped out nervously, heart pounding in my chest. I bided my time, then returned to my seat, discreetly whispering to a fellow passenger to take my father's number and call him if anything went wrong. Doubt gnawed at me as I feared being barred from rejoining the bus after the inspection.

Upon my return, the soldier questioned my sudden comeback. Frantically, I fabricated a tale about needing my charger left behind.

He scrutinised my messages, his gaze lingering on one with my girlfriend, mocking its content. I played along, inwardly praying he wouldn't stumble upon the incriminating conversation against the regime buried within the threads.

Miraculously, a call interrupted his scrutiny, diverting his attention. Swiftly, he handed back my phone and motioned for me to leave. With shaky steps, I returned to my seat, and the bus resumed its journey.

A Home Lost to Silence

As I arrived home, the weight of solitude pressed upon me like never before. The familiar building that once echoed with the joyous cacophony of family gatherings now stood sombre and deserted. The absence of neighbours, who had fled amidst the turmoil, cast a haunting silence over the once-vibrant surroundings.

The dimness within mirrored the external darkness, exacerbated by the lack of power. Walking through the echoing halls, each step reverberated with the echoes of memories—laughter, conversations, and shared moments now overshadowed by emptiness.

A Friend's Brief Respite in the Void

Yearning for companionship amidst the oppressive darkness, I reached out to my best friend who lived nearby, and whose family still resided in the area.

He responded promptly, and we shared a poignant reunion, reminiscing about brighter days while the aroma of cooking eggs filled the quiet apartment.

Before I could retire for the night, my sister called, her voice trembling with tears, much like when I had recklessly attempted to join the Free Army. I reassured her, promising to visit our cousin Mohammad's place the next day. Mohammad and I were close, and the prospect of being somewhere safer offered a glimmer of comfort.

Left alone once more, the oppressive darkness settled around me, occasionally interrupted by the flicker of candlelight casting dancing shadows across the room. Fortunately, my recent avoidance of horror movies spared me from the paranoia that might have otherwise tainted the silence. Yet, as I lay in bed, the haunting stillness enveloped me, amplifying every creak and whisper of the night. Closing my eyes, I sought refuge in memories of laughter and companionship, hoping to dispel the eerie emptiness that surrounded me.

Finding Comfort in Familiarity

The following day, I journeyed to my cousin Mohammad's place, feeling a palpable sense of relief as I arrived in a more secure area.

We spent the days laughing, sharing stories, and for a short while, we managed to forget the chaos that had become our reality. Those precious moments were a much-needed respite, a brief but cherished return to normalcy.

As I made my way back to Jasem, I carried with me the warmth and comfort of those days spent with Mohammad.

A Year Like No Other

I resumed school in Jasem, fully aware that this was supposed to be the most important year of my life. Despite everyone's insistence, and my own understanding of its significance, I found it impossible to focus on the lessons. Life as we knew it had changed dramatically, and the turmoil around us made it difficult to concentrate on anything other than the immediate chaos and uncertainty.

Escaping One War Zone for Another

A few months later, Jabhat al-Nusra, the Syrian branch of ISIS at that time, entered Jasem. In response, the Syrian regime began bombing the area, and the chaos we had fled from in Damascus began to unfold here as well. Clashes erupted, mortar shells exploded, and people sought refuge in shelters while shops shuttered their doors.

The turbulence of the conflict seeped into every corner of our lives. The constant threat of violence from both Jabhat al-Nusra and the regime's bombardment made it increasingly difficult to concentrate on anything other than survival. The nightmare we thought we had left behind in Damascus had followed us, and life in Jasem became a daily struggle against the encroaching war.

Laughter in the Line of Fire

Me, Dyaa, and Ammar had grown somewhat accustomed to the constant turmoil. We would climb onto the roof and watch where each shell landed, a macabre pastime that seems insane now in hindsight.

One night, in a moment of dark humour, we pretended to be Free Army soldiers returning in the dark. Our family believed us at first, and we all laughed when they realised it was just a prank.

(Ammar, me and Dyaa in Jasem)

Emotional Farewell

After marrying a distant cousin who lived in the Arabian Gulf, my sister prepared to leave Syria. The days leading up to her departure were filled with a mixture of emotions—sadness at her leaving, worry for her safety, and a sense of longing for the family unity we once cherished.

When the day finally arrived and she departed, the weight of her absence hit me like a wave crashing against the shore.

A few days later, overwhelmed by emotions I couldn't contain, I found myself alone on the roof. In that solitary moment, with the sky stretching endlessly above me, I cried uncontrollably for her absence. Each tear felt like a testament to the bond we shared and the uncertainty of when or if we would see each other again.

Checkpoint Crisis

As the final exams approached, the situation in Jasem grew increasingly perilous. In a bid for safety, we decided to relocate to Damascus, where Ammar's mother owned a house in a comparatively secure area. Ammar and Dyaa travelled ahead to prepare the house for Ammar's parents, hoping to find respite from the escalating conflict.

With most of our family absent from Jasem, we received distressing news that Ammar had been arbitrarily taken prisoner at a checkpoint. The fear gripped us all as we scrambled to secure his release through frantic phone calls and appeals.

Fortunately, after a few agonising hours, he was freed, but the incident left us shaken and acutely aware of the unpredictability of our circumstances.

Family Scattered

Amidst the dwindling population of Jasem, my aunt made the decision to leave for Malaysia, where her husband's brothers owned a prosperous restaurant and lived comfortably.

The allure of safety and stability in a distant land beckoned, prompting her departure from the turbulence of Syria's ongoing conflict.

Last Few in Jasem

Eventually, only a handful of us remained in Jasem: my father, stepmother, three siblings from my stepmother's side, my grandpa, and his wife—who was Ammar's mother—all patiently biding our time, hopeful for the opportunity to return to Damascus once the situation allowed.

Portraying Syrian Struggles

As a reader, you might find these details of our family's movements a bit confusing, but they reflect the turbulent reality for many Syrian families: constant displacement, pervasive poverty, and the heart-wrenching loss of loved ones—whether due to the ravages of war or the difficult decision to seek safety by leaving the country.

(Syrians fleeing their city)

Relocating

Now the rest of us were moving to a new town in Damascus, conveniently close to my cousin Mohammad's place.

We hoped for a fresh start in this area, which was under the control of the Free Army. Strangely, there was no tension with the regime, and the town operated smoothly.

We found a house right next to Ammar's, and for the first time in a while, a glimmer of optimism began to shine through the darkness.

Studying Through Strife

As the final year high school exams approached, I buried myself in my studies, particularly focusing on maths. I studied relentlessly, immersing myself in equations and problems until I felt like a genius with a heavy head. The pressure was immense, but I was determined to succeed despite the chaos around us.

When exam day finally arrived, I did my best to focus and apply everything I had learned. The exams covered all subjects, and I approached each one with the same intensity and dedication.

When I received my results, I had scored 78 out of 100. It wasn't an excellent score, but considering the immense challenges and upheaval we had faced, it was an achievement I could be proud of.

New Roles, New Challenges

As summer began and school closed, it became clear that we needed to work to support our family. My father had lost his job, and we all had to pitch in. We reconnected with an old friend whose father had opened a lollipop factory nearby. Me and Ammar secured jobs as salesmen, tasked with delivering packages of lollipops.

Each day, my father would drive us to old Damascus, where we would sell the lollipops to various shops. The work was hard and tiring; we spent our days carrying heavy packages and approaching shopkeepers, asking if they were interested in our sweet products. Despite the physical labour and the challenge of convincing shop owners, we managed to make some decent money.

The effort paid off, and with our earnings, I was able to buy a phone and some new clothes. It felt rewarding to contribute to our family's finances and gain a sense of independence. The summer was filled with hard work, but it also brought a sense of accomplishment and a small taste of financial stability amidst the ongoing uncertainty.

Intimidation

One day, after collecting money from buyers, we headed home with about $300 each in our pockets—a significant sum in Syria, especially for two young men. Worse, around $500 of it belonged to our friend. As we approached a checkpoint, our hearts sank. We were ordered to get out for a search.

In a quick-thinking move, Ammar handed his money to two women behind us, asking them to hide it. I, on the other hand, decided to keep my money with me. The tension was palpable as we stepped out of the bus, hoping the soldiers wouldn't find the cash or cause us any trouble.

They conducted a quick search and then took us to a room where an officer began questioning us. He was incredibly intimidating.

"Where are you going? Is it to that city with the Free Army?" he demanded.

We denied it, our voices shaky with fear.

He then scrutinised me and asked why my beard was longer than my moustache—a detail that could arouse suspicion. At that moment, I realised the importance of even the smallest grooming choices in this volatile environment. I stammered some incomprehensible explanation, terrified of the consequences. Miraculously, he decided to let me go. Phew! When I got home, I shaved it all off.

Lessons from a Checkpoint Encounter

These experiences illustrate the confusion, fear, and constant vigilance required to survive in a war-torn country, where every detail could mean the difference between freedom and imprisonment.

A Casual Day Turned Nightmare

Then later that summer, on a seemingly casual sunny day, we were sitting in our house. My family was at my uncle's place, in another safe part of Damascus. It was just me, Dyaa, Ammar, and his father, sitting by the balcony, watching the news on TV.

Suddenly, we heard the sound of a mortar launch—an ominous noise that usually precedes the whistle and impact by mere seconds.

This time, the launch sound was unusually close. Our hearts raced as we ran to the balcony to see where it would land. The second our feet hit the balcony floor, the mortar exploded just a few metres away from us, in the farm below our small apartment.

The sound was incredible, as if time had slowed down. My ears were ringing, and, like in the movies, shell fragments flew everywhere. One piece hit my cheek, and blood started to trickle down. It was sheer chaos.

We had to move quickly, carrying my grandpa in his chair downstairs. As we opened the door, we heard screams and cries. Our neighbour was bleeding heavily from her hand. Ammar's mother had been cleaning the floor, and when the explosion hit, the wall beside her was riddled with holes. Had she not been bent over, those holes would have been in her body.

We rushed downstairs with the other neighbours, amid the noise of airplanes bombing, sniper bullets zipping from the nearby mountain, and the cries of babies and screams of women.

That day and night were a terrifying blur, but we managed to stay safe. It was a stark reminder of the constant danger we lived under, where even a sunny, peaceful afternoon could turn into a life-threatening ordeal in an instant.

From Danger to Refuge

By the next day, half the town had evacuated, and we were among them. The mortar attacks had been the final straw, pushing many to leave in search of safety. We fled to my uncle's house, where my family was already staying.

Arriving at my uncle's house, we were met with a mix of relief and anxiety. The familiar faces of my family brought comfort, but the underlying fear remained. We spent the next days huddled together, trying to create a sense of normal life in an abnormal situation.

Paths to Higher Education

Staying at my uncle's house, amidst the uncertainty of our situation, Ammar and I hurried to submit our university applications as deadlines approached.

We each applied to ten colleges, ranking them in order of preference, hopeful for a chance at higher education despite the challenges.

Ammar received acceptance into his third choice: electrical engineering. Though not his top pick, he was content with the opportunity it offered.

Meanwhile, I had set my sights on studying English, my first choice, only to miss acceptance by a single mark. Scoring 39 out of 40. It was a tough blow to my aspirations.

Instead, I found myself accepted into my second choice: the computer institute.

A Shift in Plans

As I sat through my first lecture at the computer institute, my mind wandered far from the classroom. It was already consumed with thoughts of our upcoming journey to Malaysia, a topic my aunt in Malaysia and my father had been discussing in earnest.

The plan for my brother and me to work for our aunt's husband's brother had been brewing since our days in Jasem. Originally, it was meant for both Ammar and me, but circumstances had shifted. Ammar, dedicated to his studies and caring for our ageing father, made the difficult choice to remain behind. With his decision, the responsibility to join our relatives in Malaysia fell squarely on my brother and me.

The plan was set: we would relocate to Malaysia for a year or two, hopeful that by then, a new regime would stabilise Syria and bring an end to the ongoing war.

*   *   *

Preparing for a New Chapter

Bittersweet Goodbyes

Gathering our belongings, we began the bittersweet task of bidding farewell to friends and family.

These moments were among the saddest of my life, each goodbye tinged with longing. As we made the rounds to visit loved ones, I took photos of my closest friends and family, capturing memories that I still hold dear today.

Each photograph became a poignant reminder of the ties we were leaving behind and the hope for reunions in a more peaceful future. Preparing for our journey to Malaysia was not just about packing belongings; it was about gathering the emotional strength to embark on a new chapter amidst the tumult of war.

The mixture of sadness and hope weighed heavily on our hearts as we navigated the final days in Syria, holding onto memories and preparing for the unknown ahead.

The Unspoken Goodbye

Our departure was scheduled from Lebanon, as the Damascus airport had become non-operational amidst the turmoil. The day before leaving, my father spent precious hours with me, accompanying me to suspend my studies and attend to other official matters.

It was a morning filled with unspoken emotions, knowing it might be our final time together.

As we stood near the bus station where he was to catch his ride back to Daraa,

"Now you have all the papers with you?" my father asked casually,

"Yes." I nodded and replied,

We both understood the weight of the moment, yet neither of us dared to verbalise the goodbye that hung heavy between us.

If either of us had acknowledged it as a final farewell, I feared I would break down.

Years later, I asked him if he remembered that last morning. His response echoed the depth of our unspoken bond.

"How could I forget?" he replied quietly,

revealing the shared sentiment that lingered long after our departure.

Pensive Moments Before Departure

The next day, Dyaa and I found ourselves staying at one of our aunt's houses, anticipating the arrival of my uncle and his friend who would take us to Lebanon.

The air around us was thick with the unspoken weight of our impending journey.

A journey that would reshape our lives in ways we could not yet foresee.

Damascus to Beirut, A Stark Contrast

The journey from Damascus to Beirut, though short in distance, felt like crossing into a different world altogether. The stark contrast between the war-torn streets of Syria and the peaceful, bustling city of Beirut was immediately palpable. Gone were the checkpoints and soldiers that had become a grim reality in Syria; instead, we were welcomed by a sense of freedom and calm.

Arriving in Beirut late at night, we found sanctuary in a hotel—a temporary haven before our flight the next afternoon.

With a morning to spare, we eagerly ventured out to explore this vibrant new environment.

Beirut's streets pulsed with life and activity, a stark departure from the tense atmosphere we had left behind in Damascus. Cafés buzzed with patrons, markets overflowed with goods, and the Mediterranean breeze carried a soothing sense of serenity.

Eventually, we found ourselves on the tranquil beach, its emptiness adding to its beauty. Enjoying a meal of delicious local food, we savoured the moment of respite before heading to the airport.

Airport Ordeal

Our journey at the airport started off straightforward enough, but our optimism quickly faded when the check-in clerk noticed us. His demeanour changed instantly.

"Where are you going? What are you planning to do there?" he questioned sceptically.

We explained that we were headed to Malaysia on a tourist visa, hoping to take advantage of the 90-day visa on arrival for Syrians.

His response was a dismissive laugh, filled with cold arrogance.

"Syrians? Tourists?" he scoffed.

"You need to show $2000 each and a valid hotel reservation," he demanded.

With only about $40 between us and plans to stay with our aunt, we were at a loss. Desperate, we returned to my uncle and his friend, who had already bid us farewell.

Thankfully, my uncle's friend offered to borrow $4000 from his father, a generous gesture that could solve our predicament.

By some stroke of luck, possibly with the help of my aunt's husband's brother, we managed to postpone our flight until the next day, hoping that showing the required funds would suffice.

After bidding farewell to my uncle once again, we returned to the airport, only to face rejection once more.

Next morning, disheartened but determined, I suggested to my uncle that we try one last time before giving up and returning to Damascus.

Miraculously, the troublesome clerk was absent during our third attempt. With swift check-in and boarding, we found ourselves on the plane, ready for our first-ever flight.

As the aircraft ascended, leaving Beirut behind, a wave of relief and anticipation swept over us. Our journey to Malaysia had finally begun, marking the start of a new chapter filled with challenges, hope, and the resilience that had brought us this far.

* * *

From Syria to Malaysia

Unexpected Baggage

As we finally arrived in Dubai for our transit, a flood of emotions overwhelmed us. We had absolutely no idea where to go or how to find our gate.

In our confusion, we decided to follow the other passengers, assuming they were all boarding the same plane we were.

Dyaa and I were each carrying two thin black plastic bags filled with Kishka, a type of Syrian food that our aunt in Syria had sent for our aunt in Malaysia. In hindsight, it probably wasn't the best idea to bring it along; we naively thought it was just like a bus ride from one place to another.

Kishka looks like white powder, which understandably piqued some curiosity. Every so often, we were asked about the contents of our bags. The sight of us, two young men carrying bags of white powder, led to a few raised eyebrows.

Each time, I explained what it was, reassuring the airport staff that it was just a traditional Syrian food.

Miraculously, we managed to find our gate in that enormous airport; we just walked and somehow made it. We boarded our next plane, and the real adventure started at the Malaysian airport.

Return Ticket Confusion

Upon arriving in Malaysia, we were greeted by two large airport buildings connected by an internal train. The sight of the modern structures filled us with awe and a sense of adventure.

We made our way to the counter where we were supposed to get our visa stamps. Each time we approached, the officer asked for our return tickets. We had no idea what he meant and thought there must be another exit.

Determined to find the right path, we wandered around the airport, retracing our steps and exploring every corner. Somehow, we always ended up back in front of the same increasingly frustrated officer. His expression was a mix of impatience and confusion as he repeated, "Return ticket, return ticket," in his Malaysian accent.

Ignoring his instructions, we decided to take the train and search elsewhere, convinced there was another procedure we were missing. Meanwhile, my aunt's husband and his friend patiently waited for us outside.

Hours passed as we moved aimlessly around the airport, feeling more clueless by the minute.

Eventually, a police officer noticed our plight and took us to his office.

He asked what was going on, and we explained our situation. He reiterated that we needed return tickets.

Frustration and desperation set in as I insisted I had all the necessary documents.

Desperate for a solution, we found the Emirates Airlines office and met someone from the staff. I explained our predicament, and he looked at the papers in my hand. To my embarrassment, he pointed out our return tickets. I felt so foolish for not realising it earlier.

The helpful staff member accompanied us back to the counter. This time, we confidently presented our return tickets.

The officer stamped our passports with the 90-day visa, and we finally made it through.

Emerging into Malaysia

My aunt's husband and his friend were there, their faces filled with relief and understanding as we explained what had happened.

We got into the car and began our drive through Malaysia. The country's breathtaking beauty immediately captivated us.

The landscape was lush and verdant, with vibrant greenery and majestic trees lining the wide roads.

The weather was wet and sticky, reminiscent of the Syrian coast.

The air was fresh, the environment serene, and the sense of safety overwhelming.

As we drove further into this new land, the stress of the past hours began to melt away, replaced by a growing excitement for the adventures and opportunities that lay ahead.

Malaysia, with its natural beauty and welcoming atmosphere, felt like a sanctuary. It was the perfect start to a new chapter in our lives, one that promised peace, hope, and the chance to build a better future.

A Table of Emotions

They drove us directly to the restaurant, which had some rooms for the workers.

My aunt's husband's brother, Abu Fares, the restaurant owner, greeted us warmly. He showed us to our room, asking us to put our belongings away and come back to eat.

We quickly settled in and then returned to the dining area, where our aunt soon arrived. We greeted her with warm embraces and took a seat at one of the tables.

The plates started to fill on the table. The food was delicious.

My mind was a whirlwind of emotions, strange and hard to define.

I hadn't yet fully grasped the reality of our situation. Just a few hours on a plane had transported us to a completely different world.

As we ate, I couldn't help but reflect on the stark contrast between our past and our present. The safety and normalcy of this place were almost too much to take in. It was overwhelming to think that while we had lived through such chaos and fear, the rest of the world continued as usual. The depth and impact of what we had experienced seemed impossible to convey to those who hadn't lived through it.

A Well-Deserved Rest

After we ate, we lingered a little longer with our aunt before heading to our room to sleep, finally succumbing to the exhaustion of our long, strange journey.

We slept for over 18 hours, unaware of just how tired we were.

Our Introduction to the UNHCR

The next evening, our aunt joined us for dinner again and informed us that we would be going to the UNHCR the following day to apply for asylum. We agreed, having no idea what that process entailed.

The following morning, we took a cab and met them at the UNHCR office. We waited outside for hours until they opened, then waited again in line. The atmosphere was a mix of hope and anxiety, as people from various backgrounds shared a common goal.

Finally, we received a tiny paper stating our next appointment, which was scheduled a few months away. I held onto it tightly as we made our way back to the restaurant, realising this small piece of paper represented the next step in our uncertain journey.

Work Begins

We encountered friendly staff members and some who appeared envious, though we kept our focus and didn't let it bother us.

Abu Fares informed us that we would start work the next day, with shifts from 6 PM to 6 AM—a standard 12-hour schedule for foreign workers in Malaysia.

We were filled with anticipation. Initially, I was promised the role of cashier, while Dyaa was to work the grill alongside Abu Fares's son.

However, the next day, Abu Fares assigned me to start as a waiter until I became more familiar with the restaurant operations, with the intention of transitioning me to the cashier role later on.

The Malaysian customers were kind and patient as I struggled initially to take accurate orders and learn the menu. Over time, I adapted and gained confidence in my new responsibilities.

Beyond Work

Our exploration of Malaysia had been limited until a generous staff member offered to take us to a well-known street. As we rode the bus, I couldn't shake the feeling that I had landed on an entirely different planet. The sights, sounds, and atmosphere were unlike anything I had experienced before.

The bustling streets were lined with vibrant markets and colourful shops, each offering a glimpse into Malaysian life. The architecture, the food stalls, the languages spoken—everything was a stark contrast to the familiar sights of Syria. It was a sensory overload of new experiences and cultural nuances that left me both exhilarated and bewildered.

Separation in a Strange Land

Soon after our arrival in Malaysia, my aunt—who had been waiting for her visa to Saudi Arabia—received the news that it was ready, just a week later. Once again, our only family member there left us, embarking on her own journey.

Work Hard, Rest Never

Life at the restaurant posed significant challenges from the start. One of the most difficult aspects was the absence of any days off.

We worked around the clock and slept in the same place, which made it feel more like a prison than a workplace.

Additionally, Abu Fares, who had paid for our tickets, informed us that we wouldn't receive any salary for the first month as he intended to deduct it for repayment. This financial arrangement added another layer of complexity to our already demanding work schedule.

Longing for Home

Initially, the excitement of our new life in Malaysia helped the days pass quickly. However, as the routine set in, boredom started to creep in, and we yearned for a change.

One thought that began to occupy our minds was the idea of returning to Syria, especially for Dyaa. Seeing his longing saddened me, but whenever I recalled the harsh realities of life in Syria—war, checkpoints, and mandatory military service—I hesitated and tried to reassure him.

A New Friendship

Transitioning to the cashier role after a few weeks brought much-needed relief from standing for twelve-hour shifts. Life became easier, allowing me to settle into a routine over the next seven to eight weeks. During this time, Obay, a Syrian guy, my age, joined our team. Working in the kitchen alongside Dyaa, he quickly became a good friend.

Our Legendary Trips

As our friendship grew, Obay, Dyaa and I spent epic times together. I recall our legendary trips, as we called them, were highlights—memorable adventures where Obay introduced us to his friends who soon became ours. We explored Kuala Lumpur, indulging in Pizza Hut and leisurely walks through the city. However, these outings often meant sacrificing sleep, with us heading out right after our 6

AM shift, returning around 5 PM, and starting anew until 6 AM the next day. Coffee became our lifeline during those sleep-deprived but exhilarating times.

The Desperate Escape

Abu Fares, once the welcoming figure upon our arrival, had transformed into the typical unsympathetic boss.

Kay, a new waiter from Sri Lanka, joined our ranks. We occasionally chatted, and he spoke of working in a factory with an eight-hour day and six-day workweek—paradise compared to our relentless schedule.

Kay quit after just three days but left me his contact information. Sharing this with Obay, we both agreed to explore this potential opportunity, despite its two-hour distance.

We packed some clothes, ready for an immediate start if we secured the job. I advised my brother to stay behind and join us only if we succeeded.

Early one morning, after our shifts, we sneaked out before Abu Fares arrived. We knew if he discovered our plan, he might kick us out. The recollection of that escape now seems almost surreal.

We slipped away around 7 AM, unaware that some restaurant staff had already informed Abu Fares about our intentions.

He called me, asking about my whereabouts, and instructed me to start work at noon. I agreed, suspecting he wanted to verify the rumours of our departure. Desperation fueled our hope to secure the factory job, anything to escape the oppressive restaurant environment.

Upon arrival, we met Kay, who rented us a room in a nearby hotel, assuring us we could start the next day. Our initial joy turned into unease when he returned with a woman, demanding 500 Ringgit each—about $130—for employee cards.

Recognizing the scam but fearful of confronting him in an unfamiliar place, we pretended to agree, promising to fetch the money from the restaurant.

We raced back, aiming to arrive before noon. We made it just in time at 11:45 AM. Relieved, I sent Kay a middle finger emoji and blocked him. We identified the informant among the staff and resumed our work routine, disheartened but wiser.

Endless Workdays

Fourteen weeks had passed, though it felt much longer. Working 12-hour shifts without a single day off turned days into a relentless blur. Earning a meagre 1000 Ringgit (about $250) for such gruelling work added to our frustration. Each day was an endurance test, with physical and mental exhaustion becoming our constant companions.

The problems with Abu Fares had multiplied, creating a tense and uncomfortable work environment. What once seemed like a temporary solution had become an intolerable situation. The lack of rest and fair compensation weighed heavily on us, and the once-hopeful journey had turned into a prolonged struggle for survival.

Dreaming Together

Every morning, Dyaa, Oday, and I would sit and dream about quitting, imagining how happy and free we'd feel. We didn't have enough money to leave immediately, but we decided to endure one more month and then make our leave.

To ensure we got our salary, we had to inform Abu Fares two weeks in advance. This realisation marked the beginning of a new chapter, one where we would actively seek change and take control of our destinies, no longer willing to accept the unacceptable.

Finding a New Home

We secured a room in a towering condominium called PV2, which boasted over 25 floors and amenities like a pool and gym. The rent was 450 Ringgit per month, necessitating an upfront payment of 900 Ringgit for two months. Oday arranged to stay with friends in PV3. Dyaa and I had a straightforward plan: live there for a month and then find new jobs.

* * *

On our Own

The Guy in Blue

This scene feels pointless. I've been waiting so long, and now the crowd is leaving. I'm exhausted, tired of waiting for something to happen.

The play isn't trending anymore; people are abandoning their positions, and the value of it all is spiralling down. I need to take action, but what? "Think, think."

Suddenly, it hits me. Standing up! Confronting them!

That's what I need to do. It's the only option left.

Embracing Freedom

The day we quit marked the start of a new chapter. We were free from oppressive work hours and Abu Fares. Now, we could take our legendary trips whenever we wanted, with no one questioning our whereabouts.

We slept as much as we liked, revelling in our newfound freedom. We were young, living in the moment, unburdened by thoughts of the past or future. Late at night, we'd venture out at 2 AM, buy some chips and biscuits, and stroll down the highway, basking in our freedom and happiness. Oday brought his PS3 from his friends' place and moved in with us.

We didn't care much about money; our freedom and happiness were our currency. We survived on cheap food and had a month's rent covered. Oday assured us he could pay for the next month, and everything felt perfect.

Those days were magical. We always reminisce about them. I still keep in touch with Oday; he remains my best friend. Even though we only talk every few months, our bond is as strong as ever.

A Rollercoaster of Jobs

Days were filled with great adventures, but the inevitable moment came when we needed to find work again. There was a nearby restaurant, and to our relief, we managed to get hired.

Our new job was cleaning, and it proved far more gruelling than our previous one. To make matters worse, the boss was perpetually dissatisfied with our efforts. On the fourth morning, we arrived only to be told he had found someone who could do the job better. Honestly, we felt a wave of relief being dismissed because we despised the job.

The boss promised to pay us in a week, but we were completely broke. Miraculously, on our way back, we stumbled upon 15 Ringgit lying on the street. This small stroke of luck allowed us to buy some eggs, which sustained us until our 200 Ringgit payout came through. We decided to extend our little vacation in the room with our remaining money and soon enough, began the job hunt once again.

When Job Loss Became a Blessing in Disguise

We found another restaurant job in the heart of the city, which required a train ride and a 15-minute walk to reach. As with any new job, there was a flicker of excitement at the start, but the gruelling 12-hour shifts quickly wore us down. The restaurant didn't attract many customers, and we weren't allowed to sit even when it was empty. I would literally escape to the toilet just to sit for a moment.

Most of the customers were tourists. One time, four students came in, and one girl told me I was cute. We chatted a bit, and they invited me to hang out with them. Luckily, this job allowed one day off every two weeks. We went out, ate some fast food, played pool, and even did some go-kart racing, feeling like carefree kids again.

After three weeks of working there, we still hadn't received our salaries and had to rely on tips to get home. The train fare was only 1 Ringgit, but sometimes we didn't even have that.

One day, both of our train cards were nearly empty. Exhausted,

"Let's play rock-paper-scissors. The loser goes to the station and tries the card. If it works, call the other to come." I suggested to Dyaa,

Yes! I won and happily went back to sleep. My poor brother went to the station, but the card was empty, so he returned and slept too. We managed to scrape together some money for the next day.

When we arrived at work, the boss was furious.

"You're like a husband and wife," he snapped.

"You come together and skip together. You're fired," he informed.

Boom. Another day of mixed feelings. Should we be happy to leave that dreadful job, or sad to be out of work again? Honestly, we felt more relieved than anything. We would get our pay and resume our legendary adventures.

Among the Clouds

Days passed as we continued to hang out with our group, including Oday's friends. We ventured to Cameron Highlands, the most breathtaking place ever. Perched on a mountain, we walked alongside the clouds. The weather was perfect, with lush green tea farms and jungle walks all around us. It was exactly the rejuvenation we needed.

We only returned to our hotel at night to sleep, spending our days exploring the jungle trails. Each day was filled with the fresh scent of tea leaves and the thrill of discovering new paths in the vibrant, green wilderness. Cameron Highlands truly felt like a slice of heaven, offering us a much-needed escape and unforgettable adventures.

(Oday, Dyaa, Hassan, Bakar, and me in Cameron Highland)

Unbreakable Friendship

As days passed, our group grew closer. Oday's circle of friends included Hassan from Syria and three brothers—Bakar, Asan, and Omair—who were originally from Somalia but born in Syria, sharing our cultural background.

There were seven of us, living our lives together and supporting each other unconditionally. If one of us was broke, the others would pitch in without hesitation. It was a profound experience; sharing truly embodied the essence of caring.

In our tight-knit group, we became more than friends; we became a family. Each day felt like coming home, surrounded by people who understood and stood by us through thick and thin.

New Paths and Awkward Encounters

The days passed until Oday could no longer afford to pay for the room, leaving us with just one last month. Fortunately, Abu Fares's brother, Khaled, had opened a restaurant in Damansara City, albeit quite far from where we were.

Unlike Abu Fares, Khaled was genuinely kind-hearted. Now, we faced a tough decision: should we abandon the little life we had built here and relocate to work and live there, or should we tough it out and push our limits where we were?

It was a difficult call. Dyaa and Omair decided to take the plunge and work there first, promising to give Oday and me the lowdown if things seemed promising. Meanwhile, I found a job nearby at a small restaurant where the boss was exceptionally nice. It was just the two of us working, and the atmosphere was pleasant. Yet, I couldn't shake the feeling of missing out, especially knowing that Oday had made friends in our condominium—two girls and two guys our age—who would pop into the restaurant to greet me before leaving.

Two days before I made up my mind to quit, a comical yet embarrassing incident occurred.

On the Pakistani guy's first day working with us, as our shift was wrapping up, I noticed someone peering into the restaurant repeatedly before leaving. It was puzzling, and I couldn't discern if the person was male or female. Chuckling, I turned to the new guy and said, "Hey, bro, do you see that? I can't figure out if that person is a girl or a guy. They keep peeking in and then walking away."

To my horror, he replied, "Bro, that's my sister."

I was mortified. "Oh shit. Yeah, bro, of course, yeah," I muttered, utterly embarrassed.

A day after that incident, I quit my job and began spending more time with Oday and our new group of friends.

Friendship and Romance

We quickly integrated into our circle of new Chinese friends—Sabrina, Katrina, Sam, and Lee—who became our daily companions. Our favourite hangout was by the swimming pool on the fifth floor at night, where we played truth or dare and laughed until our sides ached. It was a refreshing change from our previous routines.

Before long, Sabrina and I started dating, Sam and Lee, both openly gay, were also part of our close-knit circle. While Sam developed feelings for me, I respected his orientation and cherished our friendship, viewing him solely as a close companion.

Life in Transition

As the month neared its end, Oday and I confronted a pivotal decision: stay where we were or move to Damansara to work for Khaled. After much deliberation, we opted for the latter.

Upon our arrival, Khaled warmly welcomed us and led us to our new home—a comfortable apartment within a condominium equipped with a swimming pool and a gym.

The proximity to a university meant that many of the restaurant's patrons were students, keeping us busy throughout the day. I juggled my shifts between waiting tables and working as a cashier, adapting quickly to the dynamic environment.

A Melting Pot of Friendship

We swiftly bonded with the restaurant staff, a diverse group of about a dozen of us. Among them were Hazem and Osama from Palestine, Mahdi from Somalia, Fadi from Iraq, and others hailing from Egypt and Bangladesh. Together, we formed a tight-knit family characterised by jokes, pranks, and shared embarrassing moments.

During Ramadan, Osama and I grew especially close. We devised a routine of sneaking out for extended breaks, taking a longer route back to conveniently miss the challenging buffet cleanup duty. Osama's quick wit always had a creative excuse prepared whenever Khaled checked in on us.

(Proving employes don't take drinks for free)

FIFA World Cup

The 2014 FIFA World Cup brought immense excitement to Khaled's restaurant. Crowds gathered to watch the games on a large projector screen, enjoying juices and shisha, which meant extra cleaning duties for us. Despite the physical strain, the familial atmosphere among the staff made it all bearable.

Misread Signals

During my shift on cashier duty, a Tunisian girl who was a regular customer came to pay her bill. She struck up a conversation, asking me how long I had been in Malaysia. Oblivious to her attempts at flirting, I answered her questions plainly, and she left soon after. Omair, who was working at the juice bar, couldn't contain his laughter when he pointed out that she had clearly been interested in me. He made sure everyone heard the story, turning me into the subject of friendly teasing.

From Highlands to Islands

As Eid approached, we planned another legendary trip to Cameron Highlands. It was just as incredible as our first visit, especially after enduring long hours of work with no days off. The fresh mountain air and lush greenery provided a much-needed escape.

Upon returning from the trip, we began to dream once more, this time setting our sights on Langkawi, a renowned tourist island where salaries were rumoured to be double. Dyaa, Oday, and I devised a plan: save money for 2-3 months, quit our jobs, and move to Langkawi. Our strategy was simple—live in a cheap homestay until our funds ran out, then find new jobs.

From Clear Vision to Clouded Plans

Around that time, a regular customer and his fiancée, both students at the nearby university, mentioned that she needed to conduct practicals for her optometry studies and offered free eye check-ups. I agreed, booked an appointment, and went there. She diagnosed me with minor farsightedness and demonstrated how much better I would see with glasses. Impressed by the difference, I was tempted when she offered me a discount. However, even with the discount, the glasses cost 500 ringgit—a significant sum.

Without consulting Oday or Dyaa, I decided to purchase the glasses, a decision I soon regretted. When they found out, Oday was upset and declared that our Langkawi plan was off. Although we still intended to quit our jobs, our post-quit destination was now uncertain.

The Great Resignation

Many of the staff talked about quitting when we did, which wasn't great for the restaurant. Mahdi, who also lived in a PV next to ours, was one of them.

The quitting month finally arrived. We informed the boss a week before, and he agreed—except for Oday, who had to stay an extra two weeks to help in the kitchen. This wasn't ideal; although we would be living with our Somali friends in PV3, I wanted Oday to be there too.

I vividly remember the night everyone quit: we sat with the boss at the red table in the restaurant, He handed us our salaries, and then we said our goodbyes.

There was a mix of emotions in the air—relief, sadness, and excitement for what lay ahead.

My brother and I left, bidding farewell to the remaining staff, and moved in with our friends in PV3. The transition was bittersweet, but the camaraderie and shared dreams kept our spirits high as we embarked on this new chapter together.

Delayed Dreams and New Joys

We were now staying with our friends in their rented room, waiting for Oday so we could rent two rooms in one apartment. Every day, I called Oday, checking if he could quit earlier, but Khaled wouldn't approve it.

Most of my days were spent sleeping, hanging out with the guys, and playing the old Counter-Strike on PC. The game was very popular in Syria and brought back fond memories of home.

Oday finally arrived and immediately decided to purchase a PS4, which was newly released at the time. This decision meant that our hope for Langkawi Island faded away. However, it didn't matter much because we were happy together. Oday and I would go out at night, sit, and talk about everything, cherishing our time together and making new plans for the future.

From Hallways to Home

At the end of the month, we found two rooms in an apartment in PV6, which was a little cheaper than PV2. On the day we were supposed to move, the apartment wasn't ready yet as they were still cleaning it. We ended up sitting in the large building corridor in front of the elevator with all our stuff.

A Somali guy named Daver, who lived in an apartment next to the elevator, generously offered us some tea. This Daver would later have some interesting stories for us. I still have a photo on my phone of that scene: all of us sitting in the corridor and drinking tea—a nice and funny memory I will never forget.

After a few hours, the apartment was finally ready, and we moved in. There were three Somali-Syrian girls who occupied the master room, which had its own toilet and shower. Another room was empty but would soon be filled by a guy from

Sudan. Two medium rooms were left for the rest of us. We had a shared kitchen and a nice balcony with a view, allowing us to settle down and enjoy our newfound freedom.

(Hassan, Oday, Dya, then me, Bakar, Asan)

*   *   *

Breathing Green

The Guy In Blue

The weight of my thoughts bore down on me as I teetered on the edge of action. I envisioned myself standing up, facing the police, and letting them do what they wanted. My heart pounded as I prepared to rise, convinced that this was the next step in my test.

But just as I was about to move, a profound sense of calm enveloped me, as if a gentle hand had pressed me down, urging me to stay still. The intention to stand up, the readiness to face whatever came next, was in itself a test of my resolve. The willingness to act upon it was what mattered, I didn't need to physically stand up. My intention alone was enough. I now have fulfilled my part. The rest was no longer within my grasp.

An Unexpected Adventure

Oday started hanging out with a boxer from Egypt named Salem and another guy from Bangladesh named Ali. I mostly stayed at home, binge-watching episodes of Friends. Occasionally, we would all go out together and enjoy some delicious Indian food at a restaurant downstairs in the condominium.

A few weeks passed, and one evening, Oday asked me if I would like to hang out with him. We went to our old chilling spot in PV2, where we met Salem and Ali. As we talked, Salem casually mentioned something about weed. I had heard of it before and knew it was a drug. Salem and Ali, who had tried it once before, shared their experiences, describing how it felt.

Oday and I listened with curiosity.

Then, Salem said he knew a guy who could get it for us.

"What do you think?" Oday looked at me and asked, I hesitated for a moment,

"Okay." I replied, Salem made the call, and soon, the guy was on his way.

Green Dreams

Salem returned with a small package in hand, and we headed to some chairs next to the pool. It was a deserted night, the air cool and still.

Oday, Ali, and I sat close together a few metres away from Salem, who expertly rolled the joints. He mentioned he wouldn't smoke due to family concerns but rolled three joints—one for each of us. They were large, thicker than regular cigarettes.

Salem handed them to us, and we lit up, smoking like seasoned smokers. One puff, two puffs, ten puffs—we quickly finished a third of it.

I glanced at Oday, asking if he felt anything. He shook his head, and we continued.

Suddenly, a wave of unfamiliar sensations washed over me.

All my worries vanished, replaced by an overwhelming sense of happiness. The world around me seemed to shift, colours and sounds becoming more vivid.

I felt an uncontrollable urge to laugh. It started with giggles, soon joined by Oday and Ali. Between fits of laughter, we asked each other, "What's going on?" Salem warned us to keep it down because of the late hour and nearby neighbours. We tried, but then burst into laughter again. That night became synonymous with laughter

Undercover Sleepover

A few hours later, we were apprehensive about returning home, fearing our friends would see us in such a state. I especially didn't want my brother to witness me like that.

Asan, our Somali friend, was more religious, and we aimed to avoid any potential complications. Our behaviour was erratic, and our eyes were red—we knew returning would likely lead to us being caught.

We asked Ali if we could sleep over at his place, and thankfully, he agreed. Quietly, we made our way back to his rented room, but maintaining composure proved challenging. Ali repeatedly urged us to keep calm because there were other people living in the apartment where he rented a room. We tried our best, but we were just too obvious. We managed to get into his room.

He had a cat that kept annoying us while we tried to sleep, but we survived the night undetected.

Under Control

The next afternoon, Oday and I headed home, still feeling the effects but now able to control them. We both agreed, as we had before smoking, that it would be a one-time thing, just to experience how it felt.

A Mexican Fantasy on Wheels

A few days later, Salem and Ali invited us to join them for an outing. It turned out they had one joint left.

"Just one joint won't do much harm," Oday and I thought.

We took a few puffs each and got into the car. As we drove, the sensation hit me. Suddenly, I imagined I was in a car in Mexico, with Ali transformed into a Mexican, Mexican music playing in the background, and everything around us radiating a Mexican vibe, despite having nothing to do with Mexico. It was a surreal experience.

From Greetings to Green

We met Mahdi, the Somali guy who used to work with us at the restaurant. After exchanging greetings, we discovered that he also smoked weed. We were at the large park within the condominium complex when, out of nowhere, Mahdi's mysterious friend arrived with a substantial stash of weed. We smoked again, but this time it was a bit too much.

As it first hit, I imagined us in a very calm place, bathed in soft lights, everything serene and beautiful. Overwhelmed by my emotions, I started running around to express myself, but suddenly I threw up.

We made sure to return home only after everyone had gone to sleep to avoid saying anything foolish. I remember coming back, Obada and I behaving quite foolishly. Oday, always hungry, he would open the fridge and find something to eat, while I headed straight to bed.

We rationalised that these were just special occasions and that we were sort of invited, which is why we smoked.

New Neighbors, New Highs

A few days later, a new guy from Sudan moved into our apartment. We soon discovered he also smoked weed, and that night, under the cover of darkness while everyone else slept, we gathered in his room for a smoke session. It felt reckless yet exhilarating, sharing this clandestine moment with our new roommate in the quiet of the night.

From Red Tea to Green Cannabis

Oday and I were determined to try smoking while walking, so we reached out to Mahdi for help. He provided us with a contact, and to our surprise, it turned out to be Daver—the same guy who had offered us tea earlier, but who we now discovered was the local drug dealer.

Lacking the skill to roll our own joints, we purchased two pre-rolled ones from him for 20 ringgits. That night, we strolled along a scenic highway, enjoying the experience of smoking while taking in the surroundings. Though not as novel as our first time, it was still enjoyable.

From Controllers to Cannabis

"Okay, that's it. We've experienced everything. Time to quit once and for all," we decided.

But then someone suggested, "Hey, we haven't tried it while playing PS4!" And we called Daver again.

Endless Orders

Every time we said it was the last time, we ordered again. Eventually, we stopped saying it was the last time and ordered every day. Dader kept rolling them for us, and we kept smoking.

Meeting the Gang

Later on, we were introduced to the full gang, which included many Canadians and Americans. They enjoyed our company, finding us hilarious because when we smoked, we turned into jokers. Unlike us, they had been smoking for a long time, so it didn't affect them in the same way.

Into the Circle

Eventually, we pulled one of the Somali brothers, Bakar, into our circle. He was the silent type. As Oday and I delved deeper into our experiences, we identified two distinct reactions to smoking: the talkative type and the silent type.

We would record our conversations when we smoked and listen to them the next day because it felt like time was skipping, and we forgot 90% of what happened.

Close Call

One day, while I was at home playing Battlefield, the door suddenly burst open. Three Malaysians entered—two men with tattoos on their hands and a woman in a hijab, all carrying guns. I was scared out of my wits.

I stood up, and they ordered me to sit down. I thought they were thieves, but it turned out they were drug police. They searched the house briefly, checked our passports, and asked if we smoked. We denied it, and then they told us they would take us for a drug test.

I wasn't sure what I heard them say, but I responded confidently, "Sure, no problem." They took the Sudanese guy and left.

We later learned that a crazy man who had issues with the Sudanese guy had snitched on him, claiming he sold drugs. In Malaysia, drug possession or dealing has severe penalties.

Luckily for the Sudanese guy, they found nothing and released him after a few days.

Oday later told me he didn't know what to say when they mentioned the drug test, but he thought it was smart of me to respond confidently. I confessed that I hadn't really understood them and would have likely said something stupid if I had.

We stopped calling Daver and hanging out with the gang. This incident was a stark reminder of the seriousness of our situation.

Addicted and Desperate

Unfortunately, we eventually fell back into our old habits, hanging out at the park and smoking weed every day.

Our addiction grew stronger, to the point where we started borrowing money just to buy more weed.

Financial struggles forced us to give up the second room, so we all ended up in one, sleeping in shifts.

Despite our friends and my brother urging us to quit, we found ourselves unable to break free.

People claim that weed isn't addictive, but that's just not true. We continued this way for months.

Oday managed to find a translation job once a week, earning around 100 ringgits, while Bakar received some money from his family. This small income went towards rent and occasionally food, but most of it was spent on weed.

Our situation seemed hopeless as we spiralled further into addiction, despite the best efforts of those around us to help us quit.

Scavenging for Cents

We were so poor that we survived on just one meal a day—a big piece of bread with some lentil soup that cost 1 ringgit. There were days when I wouldn't eat anything at all.

Even water came at a price; we had to put cents into a machine to fill our bottles. Often, I scavenged for cents around the condominium to get enough for a bottle of water. I was so broke that even affording water was a challenge. Our dire financial situation was a constant reminder of how far we had fallen.

Chasing a Fading High

Yet, we spent 20 ringgits every day on weed. It became a routine for me: whenever I smelled it and before I took the first puff, I would throw up.

Every night, I threw up, excited to smoke afterward. But the joy only lasted a few minutes now; then it became boring. We pretended it still gave us the same thrill, but it barely did.

A Wake-Up Call

One significant incident occurred with Oday that changed everything. He slept with a girl who later told him she had HIV.

He was devastated, as was I. He booked a checkup, but it was either delayed or inconclusive until some time had passed. I remember him being so down.

Very soon later he quit weed, started praying, and listened to the Quran. Now, he works full-time as a translator at a health organisation.

I stopped seeing him often—he was awake during the day while I stayed up at night. I continued hanging out with the guys, visiting them just to smoke.

A Chance Encounter

A Syrian close friend of mine, Basheer, who eventually moved in with us, was working in a restaurant next to an Arabic supermarket. One day, he told me they needed workers in the supermarket, and since I really needed money, I decided to go to their office for an interview.

The supermarket had many branches, and during the interview, the manager asked where I lived. And when I told him, he said, "There's a Somali guy I see at the mosque in that area.

Do you know him?" he asked. I instantly thought of Asan.

"Yes, that's Asan, my friend," I replied.

The manager said he needed someone trustworthy for the job, so I promised to tell Asan. When I spoke to Asan about it, he agreed to join me, and we both started working together.

Surviving the Wait

One major downside was that we wouldn't get paid until after two months, which meant we'd receive our pay for both months together. During this time, I was completely broke.

Asan lent me money for transportation and food. On Asan's off days, I would scrounge for a ringgit to buy a meal at lunchtime.

Tears and Fears

Meanwhile, I kept checking on Oday, but we didn't see each other much because of our conflicting work schedules. On one of my days off, I visited him at a restaurant near his workplace. He confided in me, saying, "I feel like something bad is coming."

I couldn't hold back my tears in the restaurant, and he teared up too.

I told him to take it easy, assuring him that everything would be alright.

Chaos in the Shop

Our first boss at the shop was nice, but his replacement was a nightmare. The job itself was straightforward: guide customers, make sales, clean occasionally—just typical shop work.

However, this new boss made it incredibly difficult. When there were no customers, he would constantly think of redecorating the shop, moving products from one place to another. We would follow his orders, only for him to say, "I don't like it. Maybe we should do this instead." All our efforts would be for nothing, and we would have to redo everything.

We never rested, working 12-hour days with only one day off per week. Although the salary was slightly better at 1200 ringgits, the boss made the job much harder than it needed to be.

We hated each other's guts. I was constantly angry at him, and he was equally angry at me. I would complain about the constant changes, and he would insist the shop needed care—but not in this chaotic manner!

Asan was more patient than I was; though he didn't like the situation, he was more easygoing.

I continued smoking every night after work.

Weeks are passing, and the problems are multiplying.

My Encounters with Thieves

To save some transportation money, a friend from the gang lent me his bicycle. One day, as I was biking to work, a Malaysian man on a motorcycle pulled up beside me and asked me to stop. Confused, I complied. He quickly flashed a badge, claiming to be a police officer, and accused me of carrying drugs. I protested, insisting I was just on my way to work, but he was insistent. He demanded to see my phone.

Hesitant, I pulled it out of my pocket and handed it to him. The moment he had it, he sped off. I was stunned and frustrated—this was the second time something like this had happened to me, the first being in Syria.

Back in Syria, a similar scenario played out. I was on my way to meet friends when a car with three men pulled up beside me. They asked me for directions, which I provided without much thought. But then, they claimed their phone was out of battery and asked if they could use mine to make a quick call. Trusting them,

I handed over my phone. Without warning, they drove off with it, leaving me standing there in shock. And now, here I was again, experiencing the same deceit.

Surviving Nighttime Threats

About two weeks after the phone theft, I was coming back from work late at night around 11:30 PM. The road was mostly empty, with just a few cars passing by.

There was a turn a few hundred metres ahead, which would add about 15 minutes to my journey home. Suddenly, three motorbikes with five young guys surrounded me, asking to borrow some money. I knew they were thieves. My heart raced as I wondered how I was going to get away.

I told them I didn't have any money and pedalled a bit faster. They kept following me, and I realised that even at maximum speed, I wouldn't be able to lose them.

I thought quickly: if I passed the turn, they'd follow. But if I braked, turned back, and took my turn, it might throw them off since it wouldn't be as easy for them to turn back.

I went as fast as I could, pushing my body to its limits. When I noticed them speeding up, and we both passed the turn, I suddenly braked, turned sharply, and took the turn. I sped down the road again, exhausted but driven by adrenaline. Suddenly, I heard them behind me again. In a split second, they were next to me. I realised that even if I continued at full speed, they would eventually catch me.

I saw another turn that would make it further to reach home, but it was filled with restaurants and tables outside. I thought I could lose them there.

I took the turn and found the road absolutely crowded with people and tables. It was challenging to ride a bicycle at normal speed, let alone full speed. I swerved through the tight street, trying my best not to hit anyone or any tables. It felt more real and intense than any action movie.

Despite the tight space, they were still behind me. Up ahead, a car was moving slowly because of the tables. I saw a one-metre gap that was closing fast. If I didn't get through, I'd either hit the car or the tables. There was no option to stop because they were right behind me.

I made a split-second decision to go full speed, hit the car with my hand to make it stop, and squeezed through the small gap. Miraculously, it worked. I didn't see them behind me anymore.

I found a smaller, empty street, hid behind a car, and took a breath. A minute later, they reappeared but didn't see me at first. Eventually, they spotted me. I pretended to give up, waited for them to get closer, and then jumped on my bike, going top speed again. They caught up quickly, and I realised I couldn't keep this up much longer. I took another small road lined with houses and stopped in the middle, completely drained.

They halted a few metres away from me. Summoning my last reserves of strength, I looked at them and started shouting at them. They shouted back, I began walking towards them, they were standing still. I started running towards them, and they got scared and fled.

One of them abandoned his bike in panic. I reached his bike and started kicking it in frustration, breaking parts of it.

Nearby residents, alerted by the commotion, began to emerge from their homes. A large, muscular Chinese man with a hard stick approached and asked what was happening.

Still enraged, I cursed at him. He grabbed me from behind, pressing the stick under my neck, making it hard to breathe.

"I'm talking to you nicely, talk to me nicely," he said.

I apologised, and he loosened his grip.

After explaining the situation, he assured me they would handle it and told me to take my bike and go home.

Tensions at the Supermarket

Back at the supermarket, one day, while Asan and I were cleaning, the boss called for Asan several times, almost frantically.

Asan said he was coming, but the boss kept screaming.

A minute later, he rushed in and opened the door so forcefully that it hit Asan. I was furious. Standing in front of the boss, I shouted at him.

I don't remember who pushed first, but we got into a full-blown fight, hitting each other all over the shop.

Asan tried to calm us down, but we were both raging. Eventually, the boss hit me in the face. I grabbed the keys from the desk and threw them at him. He blocked them with his hand and hurt his fingers.

I stormed out, and the restaurant owner next door, who was a friend of mine. I sat on a chair, crying uncontrollably.

He then took me out for refreshments, and I hung out with him for the rest of the day before returning home.

Relieving the Tension

The next day, I was summoned to the office. Heart pounding, I explained everything that had transpired. To my immense relief, they understood and reassured me. They were opening a new branch in the area I live in and offered me a position there. This news was a godsend—I couldn't stand another day working under that tyrant.

Taking Ownership

The new shop was still a work in progress. Shelves were uninstalled, and products cluttered the floor, waiting to be stocked. The new boss was a stark contrast to the previous one.

He assigned me to organise shelves, and stock products. This was the perfect job for me—no overbearing supervisor, just me and the tasks at hand.

I threw myself into the work, relishing the solitude and the autonomy. Occasionally, the boss would come in early, close the shop, and let me leave early.

After a few weeks, he handed me the keys and said I could manage the opening and closing on my own. I was ecstatic. Working alone allowed me to avoid the anxiety I felt around bosses. I worked diligently until the shop was ready for its grand opening.

The Power of Apology

One evening, my former boss decided to visit the branch where I was now working. Accompanied by Asan, he approached me with an apology for the previous conflicts between us.

"It's okay—no problem," I assured him.

For me, a sincere apology instantly mends any rift. I understand that apologising can be challenging, and I'm quick to forgive those who make the effort to do so.

A Reckless Routine

My work hours stretched from 10 a.m. to 10 p.m. Each day after closing up, I would count the money, secure it in an envelope, and then head out for a smoke.

My smoking habit intensified; sometimes, I'd light up a joint at the back of the shop when there were no customers around. It was a reckless decision that didn't go unnoticed—some customers began to comment on my appearance.

A few joked about me looking like I'd just smoked a "rocket," a slang term for a joint in Arabic.

I would laugh it off, but others started mentioning a strange smell. I played dumb, pretending not to understand what they were referring to.

One day, while smoking, I heard a voice that sounded eerily like my mother's calling my name, "Adam!" It was so vivid and unexpected that I instinctively replied, "Yes!" and hastily threw the joint into the toilet. The experience left me shaken, and I still don't know what that voice was.

A Moment of Celebration

During this time, Oday went for an HIV test. The wait was excruciating, filled with anxiety and uncertainty. When the results finally came in, they were negative. The news brought immense relief to all of us.

We celebrated the result, grateful for the good news and the sense of reprieve it brought.

Back to it

Oday hinted that he wanted to relive the past by smoking weed with me again. I don't recall my exact reaction, but eventually, we found ourselves lighting up together.

He was laughing and enjoying it just like the first time, but for me, the effect had dulled. I was just pretending to feel the high.

Civil Police Encounter

A week after Oday resumed smoking weed, we found ourselves at the park with our gang, indulging in our usual pastime.

Without warning, civil police descended upon us. In a frantic bid to avoid trouble, one of the guys quickly tossed his joint into the nearby water. Despite the lack of physical evidence, our guilty demeanour and the strong smell of weed were undeniable.

We tried to stay composed, but our fear was palpable. Oday, visibly terrified, pleaded with the officers to let us go. They herded us into a police vehicle, making calls and asking a barrage of questions. We braced ourselves for what seemed like inevitable arrest.

To our astonishment, after a tense period, they opened the vehicle door and informed us we were free to go.

We stood there, stunned and baffled, unable to grasp why we had been let off.

Did this stop us from smoking in that park? Yes. But unfortunately, it didn't stop us from smoking altogether.

The Clash with Hashim

A cousin of the Somali guys, Hashim, came from Britain to visit.

We all enjoyed hanging out together, indulging in Indian food downstairs, and having a great time. At night, it was back to our smaller circle—me, Oday, and Bakr—smoking, laughing, and then heading home to sleep.

A few days later, Asan decided to quit his job to spend more time with Hashim. I too chose to leave, despite the job being good. I managed the big shop by myself, made friends with customers, and earned decent money. But the allure of hanging out with the guys proved irresistible, so I quit as well.

We planned a trip to Cameron Highlands—just me, Bakr, Hassan, Asan, and Hashim. I had prepared my joints in advance, eager to smoke amidst the breathtaking natural scenery, thinking it would amplify the high.

Upon arrival, we went straight to the stunning tea farms. The lush, green landscape was a sight to behold. I lit up a joint and, within minutes, found myself laughing uncontrollably.

Hashim, a burly guy, wasn't impressed.

He tackled me to the ground, pinning me with his weight and demanding I hand over the joints. He intended to throw them away.

"What the hell, man! Go away!" I shouted,

struggling to free myself as he kept me restrained. I called for help from Asan and the others, but they only told Hashim to let me go without stepping in themselves.

Hashim searched for the joints, but I had hidden them in my underwear. The struggle lasted about 15 minutes, with people passing by and starring.

Eventually, Hashim succeeded in retrieving them, and I just stormed off in anger.

When I returned to the hotel, my fury towards Hashim and the others, especially Bakr, who had planned to smoke with me later, was palpable.

I chose not to stay with them and instead ventured out looking for someone to sell me weed, but it was just too risky to ask.

Upon my return, I confronted Hashim, hoping he had kept the joints. He revealed he had thrown them in the river.

The next morning, I went to the riverbank to search for them, fully aware of the futility of the task. As expected, I found nothing and returned to a nearby restaurant, trying to calm myself down.

The Guy in Blue

It's raining again, the drops relentless as they cascade from the sky, soaking me to the bone.

Many hours have passed, and I remain in the same position, surrounded yet isolated. I can't see anyone behind me, but I know they're there.

"How many are there? Do they have shields? Are they intensely focused on me, or lost inside conversations?" My mind races with questions.

All I know for certain is that I'm freezing, a shiver racks my body, a small involuntary movement against the numbing cold.

Suddenly, a voice slices through the oppressive darkness from behind, sharp and thunderous.

"Stay still!" she commands.

The authority in her voice is undeniable, and I realise how serious the situation is.

"I'm cold," I shout back, my voice a fragile echo in the rain-soaked silence.

For a moment, the world holds its breath. Then, once again, everything falls silent except for the relentless patter of rain. The tension is palpable, hanging heavy in the air as I wait, shivering, for whatever comes next.

*   *   *

A New Dawn

Rediscovering Spiritual Connection

After Ramadan in 2015, life felt increasingly monotonous. My days had become a routine blur, mostly spent playing Battlefield, stripped of the legendary trips and excitement that once spiced up my life. Poverty and boredom seemed to dominate my existence.

One morning, as I turned on the PlayStation, a thought struck me: to download the Azan app, which calls Muslims to prayer five times a day.

My religious practices had been sporadic—I often skipped Friday prayers and barely prayed.

But now, something urged me to change that. I decided to join the Zohr prayer in the condominium's prayer room on the first floor.

Embracing Prayer and Finding Relief

The first time I prayed, a wave of relief washed over me, offering a small escape from the tedium of my daily routine.

As the Asr prayer approached a few hours later, I found myself drawn to the prayer room again.

Each prayer deepened my sense of peace. By the time Maghrib and Isha came around, I genuinely felt uplifted.

The next day, I committed to performing all five daily prayers and even began reading the Quran. These actions sparked positive changes in my life.

Distancing from Old Routines

Three days into this newfound routine, I joined my friends for a smoking night but found that I had no desire to smoke.

"I'll hang out, but I don't feel like smoking," I told them.

They shrugged it off, saying, "More for us."

It was then that I realised I was evolving for the better. I deleted many toxic apps, distanced myself from toxic conversations, and embraced the sense of clarity and contentment that came with these changes.

A Turning Point in Spirituality

One night, Oday, Bakar, Dyaa, Basheer, and I were hanging out. While the others talked about usual topics, Basheer and I delved into discussions about religion and spirituality.

This was a turning point—I felt a light growing within me, a light I needed to nurture and keep glowing. That night, I resolved to quit everything sinful.

Except for cigarettes, which I couldn't stop immediately.

Quitting Smoking

I remember calling the Azan in the small prayer room, then complaining to Basheer about still smoking cigarettes. He pointed out how incongruent it felt to call the Azan after smoking.

This realisation helped me quit smoking two days later.

Finding Joy in Faith

These were the best days of my life. I felt happier than ever before. Oday would come over to the apartment and find me engrossed in reading the Quran, with joy clearly visible on my face.

I continued to spend time with the guys, sharing with them how close Allah is to us, often becoming emotional in the process.

These moments were truly unforgettable.

The Ripple Effect of Faith

My faith became a beacon of inspiration for my close circle of friends. They were moved by what I shared, starting to pray regularly and, eventually, giving up weed.

Sharing Spiritual Joy

I vividly remember a dream where I was overflowing with joy, literally jumping with happiness. In the dream, I saw the gang from the park watching me in awe, wondering what pill I had taken to be so ecstatic. In the dream I told them it wasn't any pill—just prayer.

The next day, I went to them and shared my experiences. They listened with open hearts as I spoke about the beauty of religion, the closeness of Allah, and how faith—iman—had become my new high.

Happiest Days Ever

Some of them would see me, and they would be noticing the change.

"You really look better now," They'd say, and genuinely meant it.

A Chinese guy who shared the apartment we were staying in never spoke to me.

However, one day when we both got into the same elevator, he looked at me and said, "You're a good Muslim." I was shocked, honestly,

"Thank you." I replied.

People loved the new me, and I felt a sense of fulfilment I had never known before. My happiness wasn't from any drug or temporary high; it was from an honest connection with God.

A Sincere Prayer

I realised how much I wanted to learn about Islam, acknowledging my ignorance. However, I also needed to work, and with all jobs demanding 12-hour shifts, it wouldn't be easy to find time for learning. So, I turned to Allah sincerely, asking Him to provide me with what was best.

Prayer Answered

The next day, Bakar asked me to sell his oven on Facebook. I thought he could easily do it himself but decided to help out anyway.

A few hours later, a Malaysian woman, Elma, messaged me about the oven for her maids.

She also asked where I was from and mentioned that she wanted her boys to learn Arabic. She asked if I was available to teach, and I agreed.

A Warm Welcome

We met the following day; Elma came with her eldest son, who was a year younger than me. They took me to their home—a large house bustling with maids.

After offering me dinner, they showed me the room where I'd be teaching and asked if I needed anything.

I met the rest of her family, and they were all incredibly welcoming. We agreed to start the lessons the next day.

Dependence on Divine Help

I couldn't believe how quickly everything had fallen into place. I knew it was because of the sincerity in my heart when I asked God for help.

The next day, I taught the first Arabic lesson, which went very well.

They offered me dinner again and gave me extra food to take back home.

A Generous Offer

Elma then offered me a place to stay in her maids' house for free, as the maids wouldn't be staying there much longer. It was a great offer since I wanted a quiet place to pray at night.

However, when her eldest son joked that I wouldn't manage to stay there alone because it was big and scary, I laughed it off but eventually asked them to take me back home, because it looked scary indeed.

More Blessings Followed

They continued to drive me from the station to their house and back every day. Sometimes, they'd suggest eating dinner at an Arabic restaurant, and I'd guide them.

We'd enjoy our meal, and then they'd drive me back home. It felt surreal that all these wonderful things were happening, but they were, and even more blessings followed.

Unexpected Kindness

Later, Elma suggested I stay with them in the room where I taught, and my friends could move into the maids' house.

She also inquired about my brother, who was working at a restaurant. She felt he was too young to work and should be studying, so she offered to have him live with me.

She even sent money to my family in Syria, bought me books and Islamic clothes, all out of sheer kindness. Alhamdulillah, it was all by the mercy of God.

A Life-Changing Dream

I bonded closely with her two sons, and we never missed a prayer at the mosque.

She sent us to Islamic conferences where we met Mufti Menk and other public figures.

I even led a prayer in a large mosque and attended a school to learn proper Quran recitation.

We went to many places on different islands and cities.

During this time, I had a deeply personal dream that gave me an immense boost of faith.

I was content and filled with gratitude. That was all I had ever wanted.

Receiving Life-Changing News

One year later, the UNHCR called my brother, who relayed the life-changing news to me—Sweden had accepted our asylum application, and we were going to travel there.

I was overjoyed, envisioning a future where I could study biology, enhance my thinking, get married, and help others.

Emphasising Honesty

We had undergone three or four interviews with the UNHCR during our time in Malaysia.

From the very first interview, I insisted to my brother that we should not embellish or alter our story, as many people suggested.

"Just tell the truth," I told him.

Farewell to Malaysia

The call came a few weeks before our actual departure. That day was filled with a whirlwind of mixed emotions. I was happy to travel to Sweden, but sad to say our goodbyes.

Hours before our departure, Elma along with her sons drove us around to visit our close friends.

Oday was working as a chef in a restaurant, and when I hugged him, I couldn't hold back my tears.

The reality of leaving hit me hard as I cried while departing from the Malaysian airport, overwhelmed by the blend of excitement and sorrow.

*   *   *

A Swedish Welcome

Journey to Sweden

Our journey to Sweden began with a flight from Kuala Lumpur to Dubai, followed by a second flight from Dubai to Stockholm, and finally, a short flight from Stockholm to Ängelholm.

The reception we received at both Stockholm and Ängelholm airports was incredibly warm and welcoming. In Ängelholm, some people from the local kommun (municipality) greeted us along with a translator who helped bridge the language gap.

Arrival in Ängelholm

Emily and Hanna, who were from the kommun, drove my brother and me to our new apartment in Ängelholm. They were exceptionally kind, ensuring everything was in order and asking if we needed anything.

I remember Hanna asking if we thought the apartment was okay, and I responded, "It definitely is!" They had even bought us some food and extra clothes, telling us to rest so that they could take us to the kommun the next day to apply for economic help.

Settling In

That evening, we enjoyed some delicious juice and made cheese toast for our first dinner in our new home. It was a simple yet memorable meal, and everything seemed just perfect.

Setting Up

The next day, Tom and Alma came and drove us to the kommun to apply for economic assistance. That week was busy but necessary, with various appointments to set up our bank accounts, get ID cards, permanent residency cards, and finally apply to the SFI (Swedish for Immigrants) school, where we would learn Swedish.

Adapting to the Swedish Winter

First thing to notice in Sweden is the weather. We wore lots of jackets for the first few days, especially since we arrived in January.

Cultural Surprises

Another surprising thing was how cars would stop for you when you crossed the street. It was strange at first, but we soon got used to it.

I also really appreciate how people show care, making the transition to this new life much smoother.

The Classroom Experience

About a week after we settled in, we received a letter from the SFI school, inviting us to our first day of classes. We were quite excited, eager to start this new chapter.

On that first day, we made a small mistake—stepping onto the wrong side of the street and almost boarding the wrong bus. Fortunately, we asked the driver for directions, and he kindly pointed us to the correct bus stop. As a result, we arrived ten minutes late to our first class.

Entering the classroom, we saw around ten people from various nationalities. Among them was an Iraqi man who, although a student like us, had been in Sweden for a while and was translating what the teacher said. Initially, we thought he was employed as a translator, but it turned out he was simply helping out.

The teachers, luckily, spoke English, which was a relief because we had tons of questions and often needed help with translations.

The classes were super fun. Our teacher was not only kind but also had a great sense of humour, frequently making jokes during lessons.

We progressed from one level to the next faster than many others, likely because our English skills helped us pick up Swedish more quickly.

The entire experience was both enriching and entertaining, making our transition into Swedish life smoother and more enjoyable.

All is Good

I had some nice friends from both the school and the mosque.

Dyaa and I also started going to the gym, and I enjoyed walking in nature from time to time.

Life seemed just perfect.

*   *   *

Brainwashing

Contacted by a Stranger

In July 2017, about six months after our arrival in Sweden, I was contacted by a guy I had been friends with on Facebook. Although I didn't know him personally, I accepted nearly all friend requests on Facebook.

He had recently commented on a couple of my posts with polite, normal remarks. Then he reached out to me on Messenger with a friendly greeting.

Explaining the Risks

We chatted about general topics, and he asked why I didn't consider going back to Syria. I explained the dangers involved, particularly the compulsory military service, which would force me to participate in the civil war—a conflict where I'd either have to fight against fellow Syrians or risk being shot myself. I shared my desire to study and support myself and those around me instead.

An Unexpected Narrative

He spoke of life under ISIS-controlled cities, claiming they were kind and devout, contrary to media portrayals.

Since I knew no one living under their rule, I couldn't argue based on personal experience.

Out of Context

Our conversations spanned several weeks, during which he skillfully shifted my viewpoint using numerous verses and hadiths taken out of context.

Lacking formal education in Islam and never having studied under a scholar, I found his arguments compelling.

He convinced me to share this 'truth' with others, urging them to question the media's misleading portrayals and to accept his interpretation.

The Risks of Selective Interpretation

The misuse of hadith and Quranic verses out of context poses significant dangers, as it can lead to misunderstandings and misinterpretations of Islamic teachings.

When verses and sayings are isolated from their historical and textual context, their true meanings and intentions can be distorted, often leading to extremist views and actions that are far removed from the principles of compassion, justice, and wisdom that Islam promotes.

Challenging Media Narratives

I began sharing with my family and friends the belief that ISIS represented the true essence of Islam, dismissing media reports as mere propaganda.

Clashing Narratives

When my friends from the mosque visited me, they tried to persuade me otherwise, sharing their knowledge of people living under ISIS and offering a different perspective.

However, their resistance only strengthened my resolve, leading me to believe that they were fabricating stories to alter my views.

Turning Painful Accident into a Test of Faith

I even called my father to try and convince him of my beliefs. He reminded me that I had been away from Syria for years and was out of touch with the reality there.

In a moment of stubbornness, which I now truly regret, I told him that if I was right, God would show him a sign; if he was right, God would show me a sign. That same day, while riding my bicycle, I tripped and severely injured my leg. Instead of seeing this as a bad omen, I interpreted it as a test of my faith.

Naive Beliefs

I continued down this path, consuming ISIS propaganda videos designed to attract young men. My Facebook friend praised me, calling me a true brother in Islam and urging me to support their cause.

He claimed that Sweden was part of the coalition attacking ISIS and sent me a photo of various flags, including Sweden's.

My naive belief in his sincerity led me to trust him, thinking that a true Muslim would never lie.

A Call to Action

He pressured me to generate media coverage in Sweden about ISIS's presence and their threats of continued terrorist acts if they weren't stopped. He argued that drawing public and media attention was crucial to exposing what he claimed was a dire situation.

Internal Conflict

I was paralyzed with fear. While preaching had been something I approached with a sense of purpose, but this situation was starkly different.

The internal conflict I experienced was overwhelming. On one hand, I had no desire to inflict harm on anyone. The thought of causing any sort of violence or damage was deeply unsettling to me. On the other hand, I was gripped by a fear of divine retribution, believing that if I failed to act according to what I was convinced was a religious duty, I might face severe consequences from God.

A Compromise of Conscience

Eventually, I reached a decision born out of desperation and a desire to alleviate some of this internal torment. I chose to stage an act that would appear significant enough to attract attention but would avoid causing real harm.

I planned an action that I hoped would send a message and draw media focus, but one that was crafted to be symbolic rather than destructive. This way, I could try to balance the intense pressure I felt with my deep-seated reluctance to cause any real damage or suffering.

Creating an Illusion

I purchased juice bottles that resembled Molotov cocktails, wrapped them in newspaper, and placed them in a bag. I also bought a knife, not with the intent to use it, but to make my capture seem more serious.

To enhance the illusion of an ISIS attack, I wore a massage belt from home, aiming to mimic a bomb belt. I concealed all these items in my room and kept my plan secret, even from the Facebook contact who had encouraged me. Once I selected the day to execute my plan, I waited for the opportune moment.

A Bundle of Nerves

On the chosen night, I waited until Dyaa was asleep, dressed in black with a blue jacket over the massage belt, and set out for the centre of Ängelholm around 12:30 a.m. I was a bundle of nerves; my heart pounded as I walked, and my mind raced with doubts and second thoughts about abandoning the plan. Each step was a struggle as I questioned my decision, yet I pressed on, driven by a mix of fear and a misguided sense of duty.

Echoes of Fear

Inside, I was overwhelmed with panic. My hands trembled uncontrollably as I positioned myself in front of the restaurant, my heart pounding so violently it felt like it might burst from my chest.

I fumbled with the bag, sweat making it hard to grip the first bottle. As I glanced around to check for any onlookers, I mustered the courage to stand up and hurl the bottle at the restaurant window. With my anxiety escalating, I reached back into the bag, pulled out another bottle, and threw it at the same spot, the sound of the impact echoing through the night.

Surreal Chaos

People began spilling out of the restaurant, rushing toward me. The scene felt surreal, like something out of a hazy dream.

Some patrons approached me with calm intentions, perhaps believing I was merely a drunk causing a disturbance. Others were more aggressive, trying to restrain me.

My breath quickened in response, and in a moment of desperation, I unzipped my jacket to reveal the belt strapped to me. The reaction was immediate and chaotic. Some people recoiled in fear, while others, driven by adrenaline, pressed forward.

The situation quickly escalated, and I was overpowered. They forced me to the ground, with a security guard pinning my arms and cuffing my hands.

Someone attempted to communicate with me, but all I could manage was a frantic, "Shut up, shut up, shut up," my voice rising in panic with each repetition.

My Peaceful Delusion

As I lay there with my face pressed to the cold ground, a man ran up and kicked me hard in the head. The impact should have been painful, but I felt nothing.

The security guard quickly intervened, shoving the attacker away and shielding me from further harm.

Despite the tumult around me, I remained silent, my mind spinning yet oddly at peace. I experienced a twisted sense of relief, convinced that I had fulfilled what I believed was my duty.

In my delusion, I thought that God would be pleased with my actions.

As Sirens Wail

The wail of police sirens pierced the night, and the crowd around me began to disperse. As the reality of what I had done started to sink in, I was momentarily engulfed by a strange, misguided sense of accomplishment.

The Guy in Blue

The rain beats down harder, a relentless symphony of noise blending with distant sounds of movement. Something is coming. They're doing something. My mind races with questions and fear.

What will they do? I hear the rumble of a moving object, its sound cutting through the downpour. What is this? Is it going to drug me, making me fall asleep? Will it hurt me, leaving me unable to stand?

The fear of the unknown grips me. Suddenly, through the gloom, I see it—a small, robotic tank, reminiscent of the ones in some video games. But this isn't a game,

My heart pounds as the tank inches closer. It stops near me, methodically trying to do something. I realise with a jolt—it's trying to take off the belt.

Minutes pass, the machine struggling with the task. It's not easy.

"I can take it off myself," I propose, my voice trembling.

"Do it," the officer's voice commands from the machine.

With a deep breath, I gently raise my back, my handcuffed fingers fumbling as I slide them under the belt. Carefully, I release it and let it fall to the ground.

The belt lies there, a silent testament to my submission.

* * *

The Night Of Capture

Under the Spotlight

The belt now lay on the ground, no longer strapped to me, as the robot picked it up along with my bag and carried them away. Suddenly, a powerful light flooded over me, blinding and unrelenting. The intensity was overwhelming, making it difficult to see.

Through the brightness, I could barely make out four figures approaching from behind, their faces obscured by masks. The surreal scene unfolded slowly, each step they took heightening my sense of impending doom.

Gentle Yet Firm

Despite their intimidating appearance, they were not aggressive. One of them spoke, his voice firm.

"Take off your shoes," he instructed.

I complied, my fingers trembling as I slipped them off.

"We're going to cut the sleeves of your jacket," another one informed me.

I nodded, and they proceeded to slice through the fabric with quick, efficient movements.

Once the jacket was removed, they conducted a swift but thorough search, their hands patting down my clothes methodically.

Satisfied, they stood me up. As I rose, I finally saw my surroundings clearly.

Police officers and cars were everywhere, their lights flashing rhythmically through the rain-soaked night. The entire area swarmed with law enforcement, a stark reminder of the gravity of my situation.

Their grip on me was firm as they guided me toward a waiting car.

As I walked, the rain continued to pour, each drop a reminder of the surreal events unfolding around me.

The strong light still blazed, casting long shadows and making the scene feel like an intense, high-stakes drama.

Into the Unknown

The tension is palpable as they lead me to the vehicle, the sense of the unknown looming over me.

What awaits me now? My mind races with possibilities, each more daunting than the last, as they help me into the car and close the door behind me.

In the Back Seat

I sat in the back of the police car, the cool leather seat pressing against my back. The hum of the engine and the occasional crackle of the police radio were the only sounds breaking the stillness of the night. Two officers occupied the front seats, while another officer sat beside me, maintaining a composed demeanour.

"What's your name?" He turned to me, his voice calm and measured.

"Adam," I replied quietly.

"Where do you live, Adam?" he continued, maintaining eye contact, his tone free of judgement.

And I gave him my address. After a series of routine questions, the officer seemed satisfied.

We continued our journey to the police station in Helsingborg.

Each passing streetlight cast fleeting shadows across the interior, marking the passage of time in this strange, suspended reality.

* * *

Awaiting the Unknown

Into the Cell

Upon arrival, I was ordered to change my clothes. They handed me a black sweater, black pants, and underwear. I complied, swapping my clothes and waiting for the next steps. I honestly expected something more aggressive, but the officers were calm and professional.

They led me to a small room with a bed, a table, and an iron bathroom. The details of what happened next are hazy, but I remember falling asleep almost immediately, exhaustion overwhelming me.

Sudden Invasion

Meanwhile, Dyaa was at home, peacefully asleep, unaware of the chaos unfolding outside. Suddenly, masked police officers stormed into the house, their heavy boots echoing through the silent rooms. They swiftly moved through the house until they reached Dyaa's bedroom.

The blinding glare of a flashlight in his face jolted him awake, his heart racing as he struggled to understand what was happening. For a brief, disorienting moment, he thought it might be a prank. But the stern, unyielding expressions on the officers' faces quickly shattered that illusion.

"Stay still!" one of them said as they searched the room with meticulous efficiency. "Get on the ground!" another commanded. The tension in the room was palpable, the suspense building with every second. Dyaa's mind raced, still clueless about what had triggered this intense operation.

Questions and Confusion

They took him to the police station for questioning, asking him general questions. They didn't mention me, leaving him bewildered about what was going on.

After the questioning, he returned back to the apartment, only to find the lock had been changed. A police officer opened the door and informed him, "You can't enter the apartment." She handed him his essentials before he was ushered out again.

Panic and Realisation

He was lost, both physically and mentally, unsure of where to turn. He pulled out his phone and scrolled through his contacts, finding a number for Rami, a friend from school. With trembling fingers, he called the number. Rami answered quickly, giving him his address and telling him to come over. As Dyaa made his way to the bus stop, his mind was a whirlwind of anxiety and speculation.

"Adam must have done something stupid," he muttered under his breath. Boarding the bus, his fears were confirmed when he saw the news playing on the screen. The headline read "Terrorist Attack," accompanied by photos of a man in blue lying on the ground.

"Could that be Adam?" he thought, his heart sinking. "Is that you, Adam? What have you done?" he mumbled, his thoughts spiralling into panic.

Seeking Solace

When he finally arrived at Rami's home, he was on the brink of collapse, physically and emotionally spent. Rami greeted him with warmth and concern, immediately sensing the distress in his friend's demeanour.

As Dyaa sank into a chair, he began to recount the terrifying sequence of events that had just unfolded. Rami listened attentively, his face a mix of shock and empathy, as Dyaa struggled to piece together the chaotic fragments of the night.

Breakfast in Custody

The next morning, as the first light of day seeped through the small window, a knock on the door roused me from my restless sleep. An officer entered, carrying a tray with toast, cheese, and turkey. "Breakfast," she said, placing the tray on the small table beside the bed. I was met by another officer who came to escort me out of the room.

"Time for a walk," he said, guiding me to a larger, more open space within the facility. The room was brighter and more spacious than the one I had just left.

Once the walk was over, they brought me to an interrogation room, signalling the start of a new, more intense phase of the day.

Choosing Representation

In the interrogation room, the investigator asked if I needed a lawyer. I replied affirmatively, feeling the weight of the situation pressing down on me.

They then inquired whether I had a specific lawyer in mind or if I would prefer them to appoint one for me. Considering my unfamiliarity with legal representation, I opted for the latter.

From Attempted Murder to Serious Assault

Initially, I was informed that I was being held on charges of attempted murder. A few hours later, this was downgraded to serious assault.

Although I wasn't fully aware of the legal implications, I took it as a positive sign.

Bold Answers

There were about five people in the room, including my lawyer. The atmosphere was tense, yet professional, as they prepared to delve into the details of my case. I faced them, my resolve unwavering as I answered their questions honestly. I felt it was crucial for them to understand the motivations behind my actions—that they were intended to disrupt what I believed was a coalition against ISIS.

Released and Monitored

Three days after enduring daily interrogations, I was informed that I would be released. Despite knowing I would be under close surveillance, the reasons for my release remained unclear. My emotions were a jumbled mess, and I struggled to recall my exact feelings at that moment.

Late at night, two police officers arrived to drive me to my brother's house, a temporary residence arranged for him by the kommun.

Silent Tensions

When I arrived, my brother's face fell with disappointment upon seeing me.

"I don't want to talk about it," I said, feeling a heavy weight on my chest.

"You can sleep on the couch," he replied tersely.

That night, I had a vivid and disorienting dream. I found myself atop a very high building, watching fireworks signalling the arrival of a new year. The sky shifted through various colours, and my emotions within the dream were a confusing blend of wonder and uncertainty.

In the Quiet of Isolation

The next day, the kommun called to inform me that they had arranged a new house for me. It was situated a bit far from the city centre, in a nearby town. Two representatives from the kommun accompanied me as I gathered my belongings and moved to the new location.

The house was isolated, surrounded by fields with only the basics inside. There was a bus stop nearby, but I chose not to leave the house. My mind was consumed by the unanswered questions about why I had been released. The solitude only amplified my uncertainty and anxiety about what lay ahead.

Säpo Steps In

The following morning, I heard the sound of cars parking in front of the house. Three individuals from Säpo (the Swedish Security Service) entered. They presented me with a deportation decision from the Migration Agency and informed me that I needed to accompany them to custody in Malmö, specifically Häktet Malmö.

The Transfer to Custody

The journey was mostly silent. Upon arrival at Häktet Malmö, I was subjected to a search and instructed to change into the facility's clothes—green pants and a grey jacket.

Afterward, I went through the registration process, where I was asked about dietary restrictions, allergies, and any medical conditions. Once the initial processing was complete, they escorted me to my new room. It was equipped with a bed, a bookshelf, a bathroom, and a wall-mounted TV.

(The Jail Cell)

Daily Routine

The routine at Häktet was meticulously structured. Each morning at 7 AM, staff would knock on each door, open the little door window and greet with a "good morning," and shortly after serve breakfast.

The meal typically consisted of toast with butter, cheese, turkey, a cup of milk, hot water, and a packet of tea and instant coffee.

While serving breakfast, they would ask if I wanted to take a shower and whether I preferred a 30-minute or 1-hour walk in a larger room on the roof.

Lunch, served around noon, was both healthy and satisfying. Dinner followed at approximately 4 PM. By 7 PM, staff would visit each room to say "good night." Each cell was equipped with a button and a speaker for communication with the staff if needed.

Initially, I found this arrangement ideal; it offered solitude without blame and allowed me to spend my days reading the Quran.

A Radical Reading Lens

However, my interpretation of the Quran was influenced by a radical perspective. I associated the believers mentioned in the verse with ISIS members, convinced it was the correct way to understand the text. I deliberately avoided reading other books or turning on the TV, believing that these distractions would lead me astray and misguide me.

Interview Insights

After about two weeks, I had an interview with the Migration Agency. They aimed to assess my reaction to the deportation decision. I had chosen not to appeal the decision, viewing it as an opportunity to travel to Syria and reunite with my "true brothers." Concurrently, I had monthly interviews with Säpo, where they were labelling me as a national threat to Sweden. Despite this, I remained resolute in my desire to return to Syria.

The New Year

By late 2017, I clung to a dream I had experienced, interpreting the fireworks in it as a sign that I would be deported by the new year. This dream became a central point of my hope. However, as the new year arrived and passed, I found myself still in custody, and my anticipated deportation remained unfulfilled.

New Room, Same Isolation

During this period, I was moved to a larger room that included its own shower and a TV on a stand. Positioned at the very end of the corridor, my new room marked the lonely culmination of my already isolated existence. My relationship with the staff remained notably cold. Despite their efforts to smile and be kind, I remained stoic and unresponsive, answering their questions directly without returning their smiles. Their attempts at warmth seemed to contrast sharply with my internal turmoil, and I found it impossible to reciprocate their gestures.

Mounting Frustration

By late January 2018, my frustration was mounting. "What is taking them so long?" I often wondered. The ongoing war in Syria complicated matters.

The Unending Wait

Days seemed to blend together, each one spent alone within the confines of four walls. I tried my best to persevere, clinging to any semblance of routine to navigate the endless waiting and isolation.

Bridging the Divide

I began calling Dyaa regularly to check on him. Honestly, it was comforting to talk to him, though our conversations often revolved around me trying to convince him that my path was the right one. To avoid provoking my frustration, Dyaa generally refrained from arguing too much. We managed to find a middle ground by reminiscing about our childhood, focusing on moments untouched by the present turmoil.

*　　*　　*

Darkest Days

A Descent into Darkness

As days turned into weeks, my thoughts grew increasingly dark. I began scrutinising everyone I knew, both close and distant, labelling them as hypocrites and non-believers. In my twisted perception, no one remained true to the faith.

This radical thinking consumed me, amplifying the sense of isolation. The more I embraced these beliefs, the more I felt the need to distance myself from everyone, including my brother.

Despite the comfort I found in our earlier conversations, I now saw Dyaa through a lens of suspicion and disappointment. Every word he said seemed to confirm my growing belief that he, too, was lost. The decision to cut off communication with him wasn't easy; it was a painful choice that deepened my loneliness. Yet, in my mind, it was a necessary step to stay faithful to my distorted understanding of Islam.

A Deepening Descent into Solitude

I stopped going for walks, convinced that women should not touch me when I left my room. The staff, puzzled by my sudden decision, asked for an explanation, but I offered none.

My isolation deepened further as I confined myself to my room, my thoughts spiralling ever inward. The walls of my cell became both a physical and mental prison, amplifying my sense of alienation and radicalization.

Rejecting Offers

During some interviews with the migration authorities via video chat, we discussed the possibility of living with my brother while reporting to the police station daily.

I flatly refused, my rigid beliefs and unwillingness to compromise overshadowing any potential solution.

When Säpo spoke to me, I sensed their pity, as if they saw me as a misguided individual who could have chosen a better path. Despite the genuine efforts of the

Säpo psychologist to assist me, I interpreted all their attempts as tests of my faith. My radical stance led me to steadfastly reject their suggestions, viewing each offer of help as a challenge to my convictions.

Crisis of Faith

Days passed in a blur, each one marked by the hope that it would be the day they finally found a way to deport me. But that day never arrived. I grew increasingly isolated, shutting myself off from everyone and everything, feeling utterly alone and exhausted.

One night, while deeply immersed in the Quran and my radical interpretations, I experienced a disconcerting sensation, as if my soul was detaching from my body. When I went to bed, an overwhelming sense of fear gripped me.

Despite my efforts to calm myself, the fear intensified, and my thoughts spiralled uncontrollably. I felt like I was on the brink of losing my sanity, caught in the throes of a severe panic attack. I struggled to hold on to my beliefs, convinced this was the right path.

Overwhelming Thoughts

That night, sleep eluded me. I lay in bed, my mind a turbulent storm of racing thoughts and fears. Desperately, I tried to push away the relentless tormentors in my head, but they persisted, gnawing at my sanity.

Each passing hour seemed to stretch into eternity, the darkness around me mirroring the chaos within.

Lost Sanity

The next morning, when breakfast was being served, I was still reeling from the previous night's torment. Despite my attempts to eat, my stomach rebelled, and I ended up vomiting everything I had tried to consume.

I lay on the bed, drenched in sweat, as a barrage of dark, irrational thoughts assaulted my mind.

I began interpreting ordinary actions as omens—believing that drinking water would bring good fortune, while juice would herald disaster. The sense of dread felt all-consuming, as if I was dead inside, my sanity slipping away.

When lunch arrived, I could not keep it down either

Devil or Angel?

My thoughts spiralled into an existential abyss, consumed by questions that gnawed at my very being. What am I? A devil, perhaps? An angel? The weight of these questions bore down on me, amplifying my sense of confusion and despair.

I couldn't find any reprieve from the relentless turmoil; I couldn't sleep, I couldn't do anything but suffer.

Haunted Dreams

The following night, I managed to fall asleep for only a few minutes before being plunged into a nightmarish vision.

In this unsettling dream, I found myself back in the same room, but it was bathed in an eerie, ominous red light, a camera was fixed in the centre, its unblinking eye capturing my every move.

The staff from the facility appeared, their laughter echoing mockingly around me, amplifying the sense of dread that gripped me.

The scene was a chilling distortion of my reality, blending my fears with a distorted version of the room I had come to know.

The Deepest Pain

I found myself grappling with profound existential questions: Was I becoming too holy, or was I losing my sanity? My thoughts were plagued by doubts about my very humanity. These days were the most excruciating of my life, a torment that eclipsed anything I had ever endured before.

Days of Torment

For three agonising days, I lay in bed, consumed by a relentless storm of dark and negative thoughts. Sweat poured from me as if my body was trying to expel the torment that ravaged my mind.

Even the simple act of eating had become a trial; I would vomit at the slightest attempt to ingest food. Sleep, when it came, was no sanctuary—haunted by nightmares that left me feeling more defeated and on the brink of insanity.

*   *   *

The True Me

Confronting Internal Conflict

In the midst of this overwhelming despair, a sudden thought pierced through my anguish: "If the seed is good, the fruit will be good." My current state, riddled with suffering and confusion, seemed to starkly contradict this notion. This realisation struck me like a bolt of lightning—was I fundamentally flawed? Has my path, my beliefs, and my actions been misguided all along?

The Onset of Self-Questioning

The thought of being fundamentally wrong began to unravel my already fragile sense of self. If the very essence of my beliefs was flawed, what did that mean for me? This internal conflict further deepened my despair, leaving me to wrestle with the fear that I had been misled or had misled myself in my quest for what I believed was truth.

Childhood Innocence

This realisation marked the beginning of a complete transformation. I started questioning myself deeply. Initially, I resisted, wanting to cling to my beliefs, but the suffering was unbearable.

Amidst this turmoil, I recalled the innocence and purity of my childhood. I know that Islam aligns with the inherent nature with which God created us. I needed to reconnect with that version of myself.

Childhood Guidance

But how could I do that while locked up? I thought back to my younger self and how I would try every possible option. For the first time in seven months, I turned on the TV, finding solace in a football match. I decided to do some push-ups, feeling slightly better. I managed to drink milk without vomiting, a small victory.

Battling Darkness

Despite my efforts, dark thoughts kept returning, whispering that this was merely a test of my faith. I wrestled with these doubts, resolutely affirming my desire to remain good and innocent. The struggle was relentless, but gradually, the pure and innocent part of me began to prevail more frequently.

Set of Instructions

Each time I reached a positive conclusion, I wrote it down, creating a personal set of instructions: "You are innocent and a good man; stay as you are." "Don't fall back; just keep pushing." These written affirmations became my lifeline. Whenever I felt the dark side gaining ground, I would read these notes aloud, reinforcing my determination to hold onto my newfound clarity and goodness.

(Set of instructions 01)

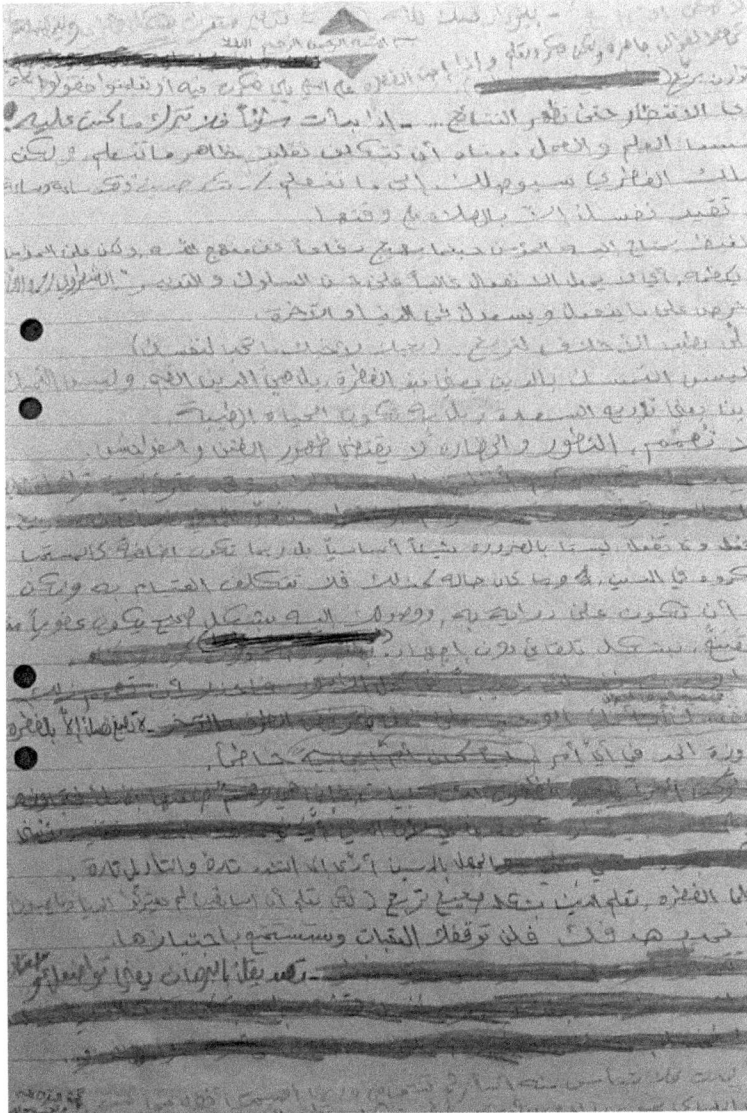

(Set of instructions 02)

The maze runner (رقم)

Don't change and don't ask wh...

(Set of instructions 03)

the Concipt of goodness contains fun, which the movies have !

open mind

(Set of instructions 04)

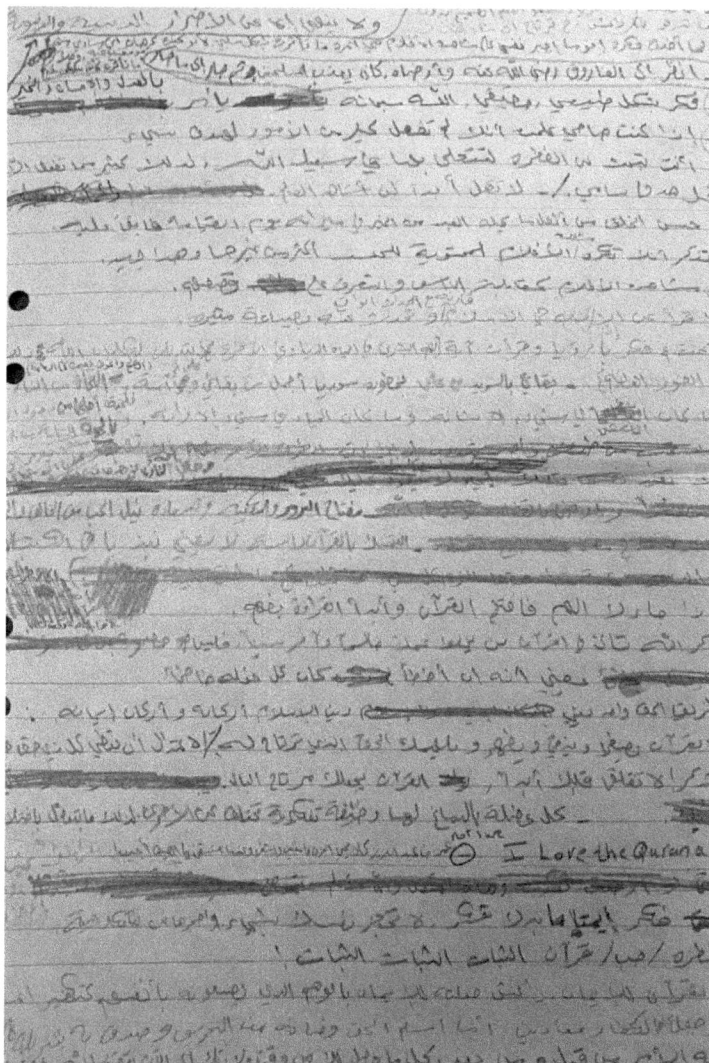

(Set of instructions 05)

The Battle for Purity

Gradually, the positive side began to gain more ground. It was a relentless fight, but with each small victory, I felt myself reclaiming the purity and innocence I once had. Although my transformation was slow and painful, those handwritten instructions were instrumental in helping me keep moving forward, one step at a time.

Understanding True Islam

I knew what I needed to do next. I decided to reach out to my brother and ask him some questions about Quranic interpretations. I wanted to understand better how I should live my faith. I asked him to look into the relationship between Muslims and non-Muslims.

He found a verse that caught my attention: "Allah does not forbid you respecting those who have not made war against you on account of (your) religion, and have not driven you forth from your homes, that you show them kindness and deal with them justly; surely Allah loves the doers of justice." (Surah Al-Mumtahanah, Verse 8).

A Moment of Realisation

Wait a minute,

"We need to show kindness to those who don't fight against Islam, even if they don't show kindness to us." I repeated this to myself, and it hit me hard.

In Sweden, we were welcomed with great hospitality. Everyone was kind to us, offering help and support without hesitation. They treated us with respect and generosity, creating an environment that made us feel safe and accepted.

A Veil Lifted

What on earth had I done? Where was my mind?

This revelation was a turning point. It was as if a veil had been lifted, and I could see clearly for the first time in months.

The weight of my actions hit me like a tidal wave, flooding me with guilt.

Shedding Radicalism

The radical thoughts began to lose their grip on me as I embraced this newfound understanding of my faith. With each moment of clarity, the darkness that had clouded my mind started to dissipate, replaced by a sense of realisation.

A Flood of Regret

A sudden thought of my dad came to mind. I remembered how I had thought of him when I was radicalised and realised how terrible my thoughts had been. Uncontrollably, I sat in the corner of my room and started to cry—a lot.

Tears streamed down my face as a huge wave of regret washed over me. "I'm sorry, Father," was all I could think, and I cried and cried, unable to stop.

Yearning for Forgiveness

All I wanted was to see my dad, to hug him, kiss him, and beg for his forgiveness. I remembered the last time I saw him in Syria, how I had held myself back from breaking down in tears. Now, the ache in my heart was overwhelming.

I longed to feel his comforting embrace, to look into his eyes and tell him how sorry I was. The weight of my regret and the depth of my love for him brought a flood of emotions that I could no longer contain.

The Devil's Grip Loosened

In that moment, it felt as if the grip of radicalism, like a devil's hold on my soul, finally let go and gave up on taking me back. It became my worst enemy. I despised it with every fibre of my being.

Realising the Damage

I began to question everything. Where am I? What am I doing here? What have I done? The realisation of the damage I had caused hit me like a ton of bricks.

I had finally woken up, and I knew I needed to make things right. I needed to seek everyone's forgiveness and do good in the world. The path ahead was daunting, but I was determined to change.

Starting with Apologies

Now I knew what to start with: the staff. Each one I met, I would apologise to. They would ask, "What for?" and I'd explain that it was because I had been cold and distant.

They always responded kindly, saying, "It's okay, we know you're in a difficult situation." But I couldn't stop saying sorry to everyone I had been cold with. I called them one by one for a talk, determined to make amends and start my journey toward healing.

A Misunderstood Apology

One girl from the staff, who was half-Italian and incredibly kind. When I apologised to her for my earlier coldness, she misunderstood and thought I was asking if she was single.

She replied, "But I have a girlfriend." I laughed and clarified, "No, that's not what I meant. I'm just saying sorry for being cold before."

She laughed too and said, "Yeah, sure, no problem." This funny misunderstanding helped break the ice, leading to a genuine friendship.

Nightmares of Syria

Despite this lighter moment, a realisation weighed heavily on me: the immense risk of being sent back to Syria. The crime I had committed and its effect in Syria, the mandatory military service, the ongoing war, and the overall chaotic situation there were too risky and terrifying for me.

This fear started invading my dreams, turning them into relentless nightmares. In these dreams, I was constantly on the move, encountering checkpoints without an ID. Each dream placed me in a different location but always with the same terrifying scenario. These nightmares still haunt me to this day.

Letters of Regret

During this time of uncertainty and fear, I began to take action. I sent letters daily to the migration authorities and Säpo, expressing my deep regret and begging them not to send me back to Syria.

Despite my persistent pleas, they never replied. Yet, I refused to give up on the hope of a positive change.

Rediscovering Myself

I decided to make the most of my time and surroundings. I started using the gym room more frequently, taking longer walks, and opening up to those around me. I discovered that I could request more activities beyond just the gym and walks, such as playing chess with one of the staff, watching a movie, or playing a video game. These activities brought a sense of normalcy and joy, gradually helping me reconnect with my true self.

A Lighter Heart

I transformed into a different person. I became kinder and more light-hearted, often making funny jokes. Some staff members weren't into video games, so we would just chat, and I found that I enjoyed those conversations immensely.

With others, I had fun playing games or competing. One memorable moment was during a Wii boxing match with a staff member who punched so hard that his watch flew off. He said, "Now it's personal," and I couldn't stop laughing.

Mercy to the Worlds

These interactions helped me navigate this confined world without the dark, radical lenses I once wore. They became a crucial part of my journey to reclaiming the true me. Spending most of my time alone, I delved into the biography of Prophet Muhammad (PBUH).

"And We have not sent you, [O Muhammad], except as a mercy to the worlds." (Surah Al-Anbiya, Verse 107).

Oh my God, the positive feelings that flowed within me were overwhelming. I cried so much, deeply moved by the Prophet's mercy and kindness.

His example had a profound impact on me. The more I learned about his compassion and wisdom, the more I felt my own heart softening and my outlook changing. These moments were pivotal in my transformation, helping me embrace a path of kindness and understanding.

Growing Stronger

In the early days of the Prophet's message, Islam was weak, with few followers and many enemies. I related to that, feeling like my own positive spark needed to grow stronger. As I read about how Islam gained strength and flourished, I felt the true me gaining strength as well. I was becoming more natural, steadily transforming into a kinder and more compassionate person.

The stories of resilience and growth in the face of adversity inspired me profoundly. The Prophet's unwavering commitment to his mission, despite immense challenges, mirrored my own journey away from radicalism. With each page, I felt a part of myself being renewed, the darkness fading, and a brighter, more genuine version of myself emerging. This newfound strength and clarity were essential in helping me reclaim the essence of who I truly was.

Through Samsittning

During my time in detention, I experienced what's called "samsittning," where inmates could sit together in one room and take walks together. Over six weeks, I met three men who were also facing deportation. I spent some meaningful days with them, often trying to calm them as I understood the profound suffering of being confined within these walls.

However, just as I would become close to one and get used to seeing him every day, he would be deported. Each departure brought a fresh wave of sadness, yet this period also became a crucial time for self-discovery. As I grappled with these losses, I began to understand the kind of person I wanted to be and started creating my own rules for my new self. This process of reflection and adaptation marked a significant step in my journey towards reclaiming my true identity.

Yearning for Connection

I longed for more human connection. In my mind, even prison seemed like heaven compared to solitary confinement, simply because there were more people to talk to. I craved interaction and the chance to experience myself with new people, but I was locked away, unable to act on these impulses.

Fear of Deportation

Days passed with no reply or opportunity to talk with Säpo. The fear of being sent back to Syria loomed over me, intensifying my desperation to stay. I was willing to do anything to avoid deportation, driven by a profound need for the looming threat of returning to a place fraught with danger and uncertainty.

A Risky Plea

In my desperation, I decided to take drastic measures to get Säpo's attention. I asked my brother to contact a man we knew from Säpo, explaining that I was in a critical condition and contemplating taking my own life. Meanwhile, I relayed the same distressing message to the staff, though I didn't truly mean it and felt deeply uncomfortable saying such things. But I believed it was necessary to make them understand the urgency of my situation.

Immediate Response

The staff first spoke with me to understand my situation and then immediately moved me to an empty room with only a mattress and a large window through which they could see me, though I couldn't see them. This new arrangement was meant to ensure my safety and monitor my well-being closely, reflecting the seriousness of my desperate plea.

Transition and Reflection

Later, they moved me to a larger room with a TV, still equipped with a large observation window. That night, I watched *The Hunger Games*, which evoked a flood of memories from my time in Malaysia. The film's themes of struggle and survival resonated deeply with me, adding a layer of reflection to my current situation.

Transition Back

After two or three days, once they observed that I was behaving normally and had several talks with the staff and a consultation with the doctor, they moved me back to my original room. Despite the return to familiar surroundings, they continued to check on me every few hours, ensuring my ongoing stability and well-being.

Taking Notice

My hope was that if Säpo contacted Kriminalvården to inquire about my condition, the staff would report that I wasn't alright. This strategy seemed to work. Whether it was due to this incident or because Säpo was finally available, they eventually came to meet me.

Pleading for a Future

When the Säpo agents arrived, they asked how I was, and I seized the opportunity to share everything. I expressed my fears and regrets, emphasising that I did not want to be deported to Syria. I pleaded with them, outlining the dire consequences of returning and my deep remorse for my actions. I requested a court hearing, hoping to make my case and avoid deportation.

They listened and then presented me with a choice: arrange for deportation or go to court. Without hesitation, I chose the court. I made it clear that I was willing to spend more time in prison if it meant I could stay in Sweden. The thought of being sent back to Syria filled me with terror. They agreed to arrange a court date and promised to get back to me soon.

Returning to my room with a huge smile on my face, I felt a surge of relief and hope. The staff noticed my uplifted spirits and shared in my happiness.

Almost Shot

My lawyer came to discuss our strategy and showed me an interview with Anna, the police officer who had orders to shoot me if I stood up on the night of my arrest. Watching that interview filled me with shock and immense gratitude that I had remained seated that night.

* * *

The Courtroom

Nervous Yet Determined

The court date was set for two weeks later. As the days passed, I experienced a blend of nervousness and determination. I knew I had to demonstrate that I was a changed person, fully committed to rectifying my situation. The staff continued to support me throughout this period, and I focused on preparing for my hearing. My hope was to secure a chance to stay in Sweden and rebuild my life, driven by the desire to prove my transformation and commitment.

Contemplating Freedom

Finally, the day arrived. The court session was scheduled in Helsingborg. The drive there was silent, filled with my thoughts and the muffled hum of the car engine. As I looked out the window, I saw people walking, talking, and laughing. Their lives seemed so normal, so free. I hadn't seen this for a long time.

I imagined myself among them, strolling down the street with friends, making plans to eat at a restaurant, and then heading to the beach. I envisioned laughing over a funny video on social media or chatting about a movie we had just watched. These simple, everyday moments felt like distant dreams.

Holding On

A glance back inside the car brought me back to my stark reality—a reality so different from what I was seeing outside. I took a long, deep breath, trying to hold back my tears. The contrast between my life and theirs was overwhelming, but I clung to a sliver of hope. As we neared the courthouse, I prepared myself mentally for what was to come, holding on to the possibility of a fresh start, a chance to walk among those carefree people someday.

Awaiting the Session

As we approached, a large garage door slowly lifted, revealing a dimly lit parking area. We drove in and parked, then I was guided through a smaller door into a stark, empty room furnished with a single chair and a table. They locked the door behind me and informed me that I could call them if I needed anything. With the court session still some time away, we had arrived early, and I was left alone in this austere waiting space.

The Moment Arrives

I paced back and forth, my nerves gnawing at me with each step. The minutes stretched into an agonising wait, each second feeling interminable as I grappled with my mounting anxiety.

Finally, after what felt like hours, they called me. It was time.

Entering the Courtroom

They escorted me into the large courtroom. My lawyer, a comforting and familiar face, was already there. I noticed two people from Säpo, the psychologist, and the man my brother had contacted. My brother and a friend were also present, offering a semblance of support. Despite the comforting presence around me, I felt a wave of discomfort in my jail-issued green clothes, with my long hair tied back. I had seen my reflection in the car window and thought I looked decent, but I couldn't shake the wish that I were wearing a proper suit instead.

Words Stripped of Emotion

I was seated next to my lawyer, with a translator at my side—someone I wished hadn't come. The translator was particularly ineffective, stripping away the nuances of my speech and leaving only cold, inaccurate words. His lack of skill made the process more frustrating than helpful, adding to my discomfort as I struggled to communicate clearly in an already tense situation.

This disheartened me deeply. I felt a growing disconnect between what I wanted to express and how it was being conveyed. I longed to speak directly in English or even Swedish, where words could carry my emotions along with them.

Crying Inside

The prosecutor began with the accusations, each one sounding more severe than the last. Inside, I was crying, wishing they could see into my heart and truly feel my remorse. As they spoke, I listened in horror, hearing about things I hadn't even considered. They mentioned thousands of photos and videos on my phone. Wait, what? I had no idea about that. It was only later that I learned my phone had been automatically saving everything sent to the Telegram groups I was in.

Lost in Translation

Other accusations were true, and I was deeply ashamed. When it was my turn to speak, my words felt shallow. "I regret this. I've changed." That's how it sounded after translation. I wanted to delve into the details of my remorse, but nerves made me forget many things. My lawyer asked insightful questions, helping to convey my regret and shame with each answer. Yet, the essence of my remorse seemed lost in translation. I wished I could speak Swedish, as my thoughts and feelings, diluted through the translator, felt like a faint echo of my true self.

What's Important?!

We took a lunch break in between sessions, but my nerves were so frayed that I couldn't eat a bite. As we resumed, the courtroom filled with more discussions and questions from both the prosecutor and my lawyer. The unprofessional translator, who seemed increasingly weary, turned to me halfway through and asked, "Do you want me to translate just what's important?"

In my heart, I was incredulous. "Really, only what's important?" Did he think some things being said in court were unimportant? Every word mattered, especially those I was struggling to convey.

At Day's End

The day finally ended, and court was set to resume the next day. I returned to my jail cell, overwhelmed by stress and frustration at my inability to express everything clearly.

Meeting the Affected

The next day, I was accompanied back to court. I tried to absorb as much of the outside world as I could, knowing I might not get another chance for a long time.

When we arrived, my opportunities to speak were limited. However, I did meet the restaurant owner and a girl who had been injured by the glass splashing. All I could say to them was how deeply sorry I was.

Heartfelt Plea

When the prosecutor mentioned deportation, I knew I needed the translator to convey my sincerity accurately. I stood up and, with all the emotion I could muster, said, "Here I am in front of you. If I ever do anything that displeases you again—which I promise I will never do—don't deport me to Syria. Instead, put me on an airplane and throw me into the middle of the ocean." I meant every word, fully committed to never repeating my mistakes.

Final Arguments

This time, the translator conveyed my message well as I repeated it twice. The prosecutor and my lawyer then gave their final arguments, leaving the decision up to the judges.

A Brief Talk

Afterward, I had a brief talk with my lawyer. He advised me to stay calm and relax, and I expressed my main concern about deportation. We also shared a lighter moment when he mentioned being a Manchester United fan, and I told him it was the team I always chose when playing FIFA.

And so, the day ended. I was taken back to jail, anxiously waiting for the court's decision.

The Verdict Arrives

A few days later, my lawyer arrived with the court's decision. As he handed me the papers, I tried to understand them while he explained the details in English.

The charges were serious assault, property damage, and serious illegal threats. The sentence was one and a half years in prison, plus deportation. This last part hit me hard.

Legal Loopholes

"You'll serve one year," my lawyer said. "If you commit another crime, you'll serve an additional six months. They will count the time you've already spent in jail, which is almost 11 months."

"Wait, so I have only one month left to complete the year?" I asked, feeling a glimmer of hope.

"Unfortunately, all the time you've spent before the court decision was under migration custody, so it doesn't count."

"Wait, what?! Those 10 months don't count? That's just unfair! I was in jail anyway. Why would it matter if it was under migration or police custody?"

"That's the law, unfortunately. So, you have 11 months remaining now."

I was frustrated. Eleven months felt like an eternity, being just alone between four walls. But at least I would be in prison, where there would be people to talk to. The deportation was what truly worried me.

"What happens now?" I asked.

"You wait around a week or two until you're moved to prison," he replied.

Between a Rock and a Hard Place

Two more weeks in this solitary confinement felt unbearable. I was desperate to get out of there, but the looming deportation kept gnawing at my mind. Should I appeal? It would mean waiting an extra month, and I was already extremely exhausted from waiting. Plus, what if they increased my sentence?

I was stuck with these thoughts, unsure of what to do. I was tempted to appeal solely because of the deportation, but I just couldn't bear one more hour here. I was utterly exhausted in jail and didn't want to sink into deeper despair.

A Painful Choice

After much internal struggle and consultation with my lawyer, I decided not to appeal. I hoped we could find a solution for the deportation later.

Missed Opportunity

Later, I discovered that I could have appealed the deportation decision separately, leaving the prison sentence as it was. I couldn't believe my lawyer hadn't mentioned this option. By the time I learned about it, the appeal period had already passed. I was deeply disappointed.

Counting Down

The final days in jail seemed to stretch on forever. I had spent countless hours imagining what prison life would be like, crafting scenarios in my mind to pass the time.

Stuck in Limbo

Two weeks had drifted by, and still, there was no sign of my transfer. Doubts began to creep in—had they changed their minds and decided to keep me here indefinitely? My mind raced with questions, each one adding to the growing strain of my confinement.

To pass the time, I engaged in whatever activities I could: reading, walking, watching TV, and chatting with the staff. In a place like this, you constantly need to find something to do because emptiness kills.

Turning the Page

Finally, a week after the interminable two weeks, I received the news I had been yearning for—I was moving to prison. The joy that surged through me was almost beyond words. As I prepared to leave, I took a moment to say goodbye to the staff who had been a part of my daily life. Their well-wishes were heartfelt, and as I left, I felt a pang of sadness. There were even tears in my eyes as I parted ways with some of them.

I had spent a year in that place, a year filled with intense experiences and extreme emotions. In that time, A dark me died and a bright me was born.

The struggles, the tears, and the triumphs had transformed me.

Now, as I prepared to step into a new environment, it felt like a fresh start—an opportunity to see how this next phase of my journey would unfold.

* * *

Behind the Barbed Wire

First Impressions

Far from the bustle of the city stood the prison, a solitary structure encircled by barbed wire, with no homes or apartments in sight. It was October 2018, and at the age of 22, I arrived at noon on a surprisingly sunny day. As I approached the prison gates, the reality of my situation began to sink in.

The initial process was a series of formalities: a thorough search, a change of clothes, and a urine test to ensure there were no drugs in my system.

A Glimpse of Independence

After that, I was moved to a room in a corridor with three rooms. It was similar to my jail cell, except this one had a bathroom door that I could lock. To my surprise, after showing me the room, the staff left without locking the door. I thought it was a mistake.

"Hello sir, the door is still open. I can just leave." But it was intentional—a huge first advantage. I could enter and exit my room whenever I wanted. Even though it only led to a small corridor, it made me feel so happy.

A Shared Space

In the corridor, there were two tables where we could eat and converse with the other inmates, along with a small shared fridge that proved quite handy. The setup was a significant upgrade from my previous confinement. One of the rooms was empty, while the adjacent room housed an inmate serving time for drug-related offences.

Though we exchanged a few pleasantries and got to know each other a bit, he mostly preferred to stay in his room, engrossed in watching TV. In contrast, I was eager to engage with others and make the most of the social opportunities presented by our shared space.

Bonding Beyond Backgrounds

When it was time for my first walk in the prison yard, the experience was nothing short of astounding. The yard was an open space adorned with plants you could actually touch and a patch of ground where you could sit. It was a rare touch of beauty and nature that felt almost liberating.

During this walk, two other inmates from the adjacent corridor joined us: a Swedish citizen of African descent and another man with a Senegalese father and an Israeli mother, Yamien. I just wanted to make friends, no longer caring about backgrounds. I quickly struck up a friendship with Yamien, and we would walk together and talk about different matters.

Excitement Builds

I kept asking them about the actual prison, where we would move once rooms were available. There, I learned, were more staff and inmates, and we would have "light work" to do. I was excited about the larger communal spaces, where inmates could watch TV, play chess, or engage in board games. All of it sounded thrilling, and I couldn't wait for a room to become available for me.

Ready to Move

Around two weeks later, after having met a few new inmates and settled into a routine, the moment finally arrived for me to move. The anticipation had been building, and I was brimming with excitement.

A Change in Oversight

Accompanied by two staff members, I headed upstairs to what looked like a big living room. It had blue couches, two TVs, one with a 360 Xbox, two tables with chairs, and a small office where 1-2 staff members were stationed. What struck me as strange was that this single staff member oversaw many inmates, a stark contrast to my previous situation where I was always accompanied by one or two staff members.

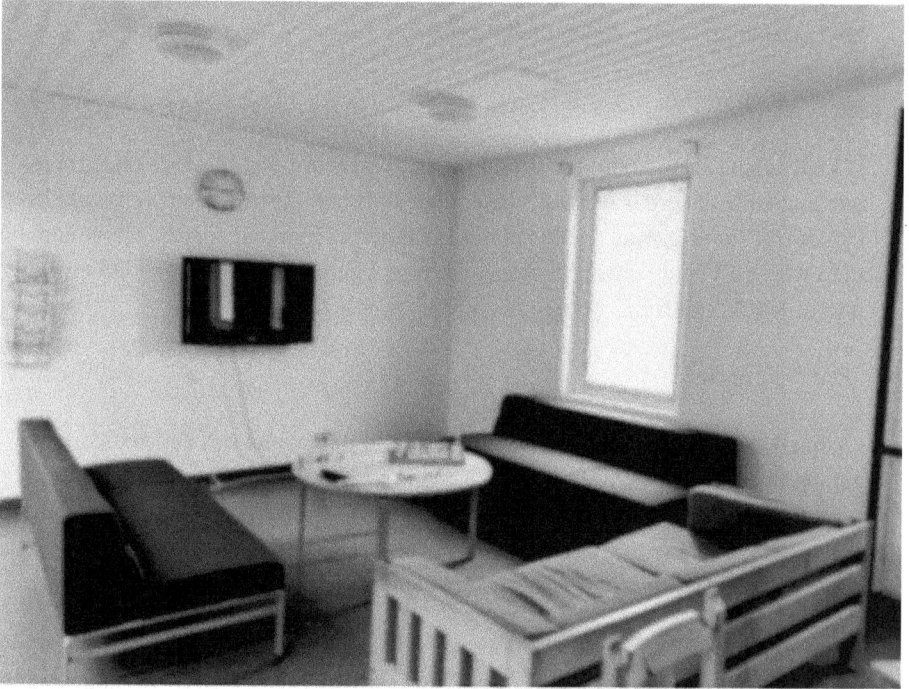

(One half of the prison common room)

Settling In

I was given a key and taken to my room, which resembled the one downstairs but had an unpleasant odour. Later, I learned the previous occupant had been pelted with eggs on his last day—a prison tradition. He hadn't done a great job cleaning up, so my first task was to clean the room. Once that was done, I set up my bed and tried to get a feel for the place.

Navigating New Territory

Arriving in a new area with no familiar faces, I found the atmosphere quite intimidating. Some inmates had a tough demeanour, marked by bald heads and intricate tattoos, while others seemed more approachable. Determined to make the best of it, I set out to explore my new surroundings.

We were on the second floor, which housed a corridor with five rooms, a shower, and a spacious kitchen equipped with a fridge, microwave, and toaster. The floor was organised into four corridors—two on each side—centering around a larger common room and the office. In total, there were 20 inmates on our floor, with another 20 on the first floor. We'd interact with the first-floor inmates mainly during work hours or in the dining room.

Making Connections

Feeling somewhat oriented, I took a seat in the common room, where I soon met an inmate, Jaw, who was more outgoing. He initiated the usual questions: "What are you in for? How did you live before?" I chose to keep my responses vague, mentioning "property damage and serious assault," and noted that I was from Helsingborg.

Previously, when I said I was from Ängelholm, someone connected me to the terrorist attack, so I decided to stick with Helsingborg to avoid suspicion.

Cosy Dining Room

As dinner approached, all the inmates gathered in front of the locked door by the stairs, eagerly awaiting the staff to unlock it. Once the door was opened, we formed a line in the long corridor downstairs and made our way into the dining room.

To my surprise, the dining room was surprisingly cosy. It was filled with the sounds of animated conversations and laughter, creating a vibrant and welcoming atmosphere. The lively interactions among the inmates made the space feel surprisingly warm and communal, offering a glimpse into the more social side of prison life.

Dinner Dynamics

At dinner time, two staff members were on duty—one inside the dining room keeping watch, and the other stationed by the door. We each grabbed a tray and plate, which were then filled by the cook's assistant. With our trays loaded, we selected a table to sit at.

Jaw from earlier invited me to join his table, where I ended up sitting with him and four others. The conversation was sparse, with only the occasional exchange of glances and nods breaking the silence. Despite the quiet company, I appreciated the familiar taste of the Swedish healthy meal. It was a comforting start to my new routine, offering a small sense of normalcy amid the changes.

From Dinner to Basketball

After dinner, I headed back to the floor, and it wasn't long before it was time for gym access. The gym featured a small, enclosed futsal area equipped with two goals and two basketball hoops. I joined two other inmates for a game of basketball, relishing the opportunity to stretch my legs and partake in some friendly competition.

Maximising the Evening

We had an hour there before needing to return to our floor. After our workout, we came back with about 1 hour to spare before the corridors were locked for the night. I seized this opportunity to take a refreshing shower, and connect more with others, making the most of the remaining time.

End of the Day

By 7 pm, the corridors were locked, and by 7:10 pm, we were required to be in our rooms, which would remain locked until 7 am the following day. As I settled into my cell for the night, reflecting on my first day in prison, I found it surprisingly manageable. Despite the unfamiliar environment and the gravity of my situation, the day had been filled with small adjustments and moments of connection that made the transition feel bearable.

A Quiet Start

By the next morning, once the rooms were unlocked, I headed to our corridor kitchen and grabbed some milk and toast. The quiet morning routine brought a welcome sense of normalcy. After breakfast, I made my way to the common room, carrying a book on general management. The room was peaceful, as most inmates were at work, allowing me to settle into a corner and immerse myself in reading.

Observing Routine

With work assignments still a few days away for me, I had time to observe the daily rhythm of the prison. Before lunch, the inmates returned from their morning tasks, and we headed to the dining room together. Afterward, we had an hour-long walk in a large football yard. The yard was a vibrant hub of activity, with groups playing football, sitting, or just walking. Smokers took advantage of the break, but since I didn't smoke, I enjoyed the walk without the added stress.

Breaking Barriers

I primarily spoke English with everyone. Although I could manage in Swedish, English was my go-to for easier communication. After the walk, the inmates went back to work for another three hours, returning later for dinner. As the days passed, I began to make friends. The guys who initially seemed unapproachable turned out to be friendly and welcoming.

Evening Basketball

In the evenings, I joined some inmates for basketball. The court was a lively place, filled with laughter and camaraderie. The routine of my days started to feel fulfilling. The structured schedule, the friendly interactions, and the physical activity helped me find a sense of contentment in this new environment.

Rejoining Jumu'ah Prayers

Friday came, and I learned that an imam visited for the Friday prayer. Those who wanted to join could go with him to the prayer room, a shared space for both the imam and the priest's gatherings. Opting to join the prayer meant missing the outside walk, but I didn't mind because I knew the importance of Jumu'ah.

Walking with him and a few other inmates to the prayer room, I felt tears in my eyes, having missed Jumu'ah prayers for an entire year while in jail. This moment was profoundly emotional.

A Tranquil Gathering

When we arrived at the prayer room, we had some time before the prayer began. The imam answered questions from the inmates. Afterward, we prepared the room for the Friday Khutba and the subsequent prayer. The atmosphere was peaceful and soothing, and I felt a deep sense of relief and happiness.

Weekend Fun

The next day was Saturday, a break from the usual work routine. This gave me a chance to engage more with the other inmates. We spent the day playing chess and organising a FIFA tournament on Xbox. The room buzzed with excitement and laughter as we competed and bonded over the games.

In the evening, we played football in the futsal court. I hadn't run this much in a long time, and it felt exhilarating. I was drenched in sweat, and the shower afterward was incredibly refreshing. The weekend passed quickly but was filled with camaraderie.

Starting Work

The following week, I was assigned to the carpentry workshop. Joining the others in the morning, I found the environment to be quite relaxed. We learned to make bottle boxes, taking frequent breaks to chat and stretch. It was a low-pressure setting, perfect for those who didn't want to exert themselves too much. Some inmates would half-heartedly comply when the staff asked them to work, but they mostly just sat around. I, on the other hand, didn't mind working. It was engaging and gave me something to focus on.

Uncle Othman's Permission

In the carpentry workshop, I met an elderly Somali man who was incredibly kind. We became close friends over time. Everyone called him Ammo, which means uncle. We had a running joke where we pretended not to do anything unless Uncle Othman gave us permission. If the staff asked us to work, we would consult Uncle Othman first.

The Inmate Landscape

I met many people and heard countless stories. Most inmates were there for minor offences like drugs or theft, though there were a few cases involving more serious crimes like kidnapping and gun possession. Most had shorter sentences compared to mine—just a few months—and would move to Class 3 when they had about a month remaining.

Class 3 was described as more of an open prison. It became evident that I would be among the longest-staying inmates in this group, giving me ample time to forge connections and adapt to this new chapter in my life.

A Curious Glance

One morning, as I was heading to work as usual, I noticed one of the staff members, Norah, looking at me. It was a curious glance, almost as if she had a crush on me. Unsure if it was my imagination, I continued with my routine. I made my morning coffee, sat for about 15 minutes, and then started working.

Dangerous Fun

Some inmates would mess around with air guns and staples, shooting at each other. It was dangerous, so I made it a point to avoid these risky games, especially since they only occurred when no staff were around. The thrill of these impromptu fights was overshadowed by the potential for injury, making it wise to stay clear of such reckless behaviour.

Casual Chats and Hidden Feelings

Later that day, after dinner, I was in the common room when Norah came and sat at my table. She struck up a casual conversation, and I went along with it. We asked each other good questions and got to know one another. Norah was a Swedish girl, a year younger than me, beautiful and smart. Our conversations became frequent, and while we didn't openly show our feelings, it was clear we liked each other.

Chess and Camaraderie

As days passed, I got to know the other inmates better. I helped new arrivals who seemed as lost as I had been on my first day. We said goodbye to many and welcomed new faces. One guy, Uyyub, who arrived after me, became a close friend, along with Uncle Othman. We spent most of our time together, both at work and on our floor. Uyyub was a master chess player, and he taught me a lot. With his techniques, I became quite good at the game.

The Fine Line

My relationship with all the inmates grew strong. Everyone liked and respected me, and I treated them with the same respect. Even the staff liked me, and I found it important to balance these two relationships. If someone seemed too close to the staff, the inmates would accuse him of being a snitch, and snitches got beaten. I saw this happen to two guys; they were beaten with wooden chairs, and we were all locked in our rooms for four days.

Conflicting Loyalties

Days passed, and the routine remained the same. New people came, and older ones left. A few days before the Yameen was about to be released, he became extremely angry with Jaw, who often made silly jokes. While at work, he confided in me that he wanted to beat Jaw and hurt him badly. I felt stuck—telling Jaw would mean losing the Yameen 's respect, but I also didn't want anyone to get hurt.

Bridging Conflict:

I reminded him that he only had a few days left until his release and mentioned his little daughter, trying to calm him down. I said, "Your daughter is waiting for you. Don't make her wait any longer." Thankfully, this worked, and he eventually calmed down. I tried to solve as many disputes as possible because there was always tension between inmates, and I hated seeing fights. Maybe it was because of what I went through—from extreme violence to a desire for peace and calm.

Books and Lessons

As the days passed, I made the most of my time by getting lots of books from the library on library day. I read on various topics: self-improvement, biology, and the Quran with the right understanding. Uyyub and Uncle Othman wanted to learn Arabic, so I used the weekends to gather them around the table in our corridor kitchen and teach them Arabic there.

Breaking Language Barriers

A guy from Congo who recently arrived spoke only French, with very little English. He was a priest, in for something minor that I'd rather not mention, and had a short sentence. Despite the language barrier, we became quite close. I knew only a little French, so I started learning from him. I'd take my papers and pens, learning French while teaching him English.

The staff even called me to translate for him, thinking I was fluent in French. Because of our close bond, I could usually understand what he wanted.

Six Months In

By now, I'd been in prison for about six months. Not much had changed; the same routine repeated itself. I longed for freedom and counted the days. No matter how many things you have, when you lack freedom, you have nothing. During these six months, we were locked in our rooms three times, each for three to four days. This usually happened because of fights with the staff or between inmates.

They would lock everyone up and conduct investigations. There were no cameras except in the futsal court and at work.

Anxiety of Uncertain Futures

It was June now, and summer had started. I had two months left until my release, but anxiety often crept in. I couldn't appeal my deportation because the time had passed, and I was now in contact with a new lawyer, having replaced my previous one. I feared that once my time here was up, I'd be moved back to custody and face endless waiting as they tried to find another way. This idea terrified me, and I still had nightmares about Syria. To keep my mind off it, I tried to fill my days as much as possible.

My Decision to Distance from Norah

Uncertainty about my future led me to distance myself from Norah. I was concerned about the potential risks if circumstances turned against us, so I decided it was best to keep a low profile. About three weeks later, Norah seemed to have quit, as I no longer saw her around.

In her place, new staff members had joined for summer jobs, including two girls who frequently glanced in my direction. Despite their attention, I chose to remain focused on other aspects of my life and keep my mind occupied with various activities.

Barbecue Bliss

Summer brought some relief with monthly barbecues in the big open football court. These events felt like mini-holidays. In June, we had our first barbecue. We enjoyed grilled burgers and hotdogs, and then played football in the big field. We formed two teams, and I played on defence. Although I wasn't particularly skilled, I managed to halt a few attacks and contribute to the game. The barbecue and the subsequent match provided a much-needed distraction and lifted our spirits, making it a truly enjoyable day that eased many of our worries.

Counting Down

Now it's July, and I'm counting the days. Each week, I mark small events on my calendar, telling myself, "This week we have this, it'll go fast. Next week we have that, it'll go fast too." The mix of excitement and nervousness keeps me on edge. I've become the longest-serving inmate here. Everyone knows me and respects me, which makes it easier to resolve disputes since I've been here the longest.

Swedish Surprises

I remember my last two weeks when I started speaking Swedish more often. Both staff and inmates were amazed. They'd say, "Bro, you speak good Swedish, why do you speak in English?" I'd reply, "You know, it's easier for me to communicate in English." They'd laugh and say, "Screw that, man, speak Swedish with us!"

Beyond Stereotypes

I've realised that inmates who have committed crimes are not fundamentally different from others. Among them, there are many genuinely kind and decent people. Conversely, some of the staff members exhibit quite a bit of arrogance.

Need for Acceptance

When inmates leave prison, finding a job becomes a daunting challenge due to background checks. Many inmates express that their time in prison is their first and last, showing genuine regret for their past actions. It's clear that society's acceptance and support are crucial in helping them secure decent employment.

Providing job opportunities could significantly reduce the likelihood of reoffending, offering a fresh start for those who have genuinely turned a new leaf. I hope this perspective gains more discussion and attention, as it's essential for fostering rehabilitation and reintegration.

Ten Days to Go

With just ten days remaining, my anxiety has reached its peak. I find myself constantly on the phone with my lawyer, trying to stay calm and focused. Each conversation is a mix of hope and nervousness as I navigate these final, tense moments before my release.

Overwhelmed with Relief

Three days later, I receive incredible news that fills me with indescribable joy. The migration authorities have suspended my deportation, and I'm told I will be released. I break down in tears of happiness, overwhelmed by the relief and hope this news brings.

A Heartfelt Compliment

With only two days remaining, I remember having a chat with one of the staff members. He told me, "You know, the staff were discussing the inmates, and they singled you out as the best—remarkably kind and helpful." Hearing that made me genuinely happy.

Neighbourly Bonds

I had earned much respect and affection from the inmates as well. Some would say, "Adam is the smartest here, always reading books," while others would come to me with their dreams, asking if I could interpret them.

Next to my room, there was a guy named Antoni who occasionally asked for some juice from my concentrated juice bottle in the fridge. I always obliged, telling him, "Take it, no problem." Eventually, I told him, "Just open the fridge and take what you want. You don't need to ask me." He would respond with gratitude, calling me "the best neighbours ever." Antoni was there for drug use, a simple man with a kind heart.

A Clean Record

Some asked me how many reports I had received. Reports were given for any misbehaviour or illegal activities. I told him, "None—zero here and zero back in custody." They were surprised, as each one of them had at least three.

Additionally, the staff informed me that due to my good behaviour, I wouldn't need to attend the usual post-prison interviews by Kriminalvården to check on my progress. When the guy from Säpo read this, he remarked, "This is really good."

Solace in Positivity

In this environment, where positivity was not just a fleeting sentiment but a daily practice, I found solace. These exchanges, alongside the friendships nurtured with individuals, enriched my days and underscored the resilience and humanity within these walls.

Revealing My Past

I shared the details of my crime with five people: Ayyub, Uncle Othman, Norah, and two others. Their reactions varied, with some expressing surprise and disbelief. They couldn't reconcile the person they knew with the gravity of my past actions, and a few even thought I was lying. The contrast between my current self and my previous actions was striking to them, highlighting how far I had come since those months.

Bittersweet Farewells

Now it was time to say my goodbyes, thankfully, the tradition of throwing eggs at departing inmates was no longer practised. Instead, the current tradition was to buy cakes for the inmates, so I made sure to do that. Saying goodbye was tough; I had formed close relationships with many, and farewells are always difficult. I've had to say many goodbyes in my life to people I never saw again, and this was no different.

The Last Sunset

The night before my final morning, as I returned to my room for the last time after meticulously cleaning it, reality hit me hard. The room, once filled with the constant hum of my daily routines, now stood silent and empty, echoing my mixed emotions. This was my last night in this place—a place that had become both a prison and a peculiar home. Tomorrow, the door to my freedom will finally open.

The Morning of Liberation

I woke up that morning, a blend of excitement and nerves coursing through me. The future was a mystery, but I was ready. My room, prepared for the next occupant, felt like a chapter closing. Stepping into the common room, I saw the familiar faces of inmates heading to work. I exchanged final goodbyes, each one heavy words.

The Moment of Truth

An hour later, the staff arrived, signalling it was time. They escorted me downstairs, where I changed into the clothes my brother had brought me. Just wearing them made me feel like a different person, filled with anticipation. There was no hint of further lockup, which heightened my excitement.

Final Checkpoint

I was taken to the visiting room, where two agents from Säpo were waiting. They asked how I was doing and handed me a decision notice: my deportation was still on hold, but I had to report to the police station every day to prove I was still in Sweden. I had no issue with that. They asked who would pick me up, and I told them it was my brother and friends. After they left, the staff made sure I had all my belongings and walked me to the main door.

*   *   *

The Threshold of Freedom

Tears of Liberation

As they opened it and told me I was free to go, I hesitated. "Wait, are you not going to keep walking with me?" For 22 months, I had never walked alone through a door. The feeling was indescribable—walking alone, with the staff wishing me "lycka till" (good luck) as I approached the outer gate. Tears welled up in my eyes as I stepped outside. For the first time, no one was directing me, and the feeling of absolute freedom was beyond anything I had ever imagined.

Savouring Freedom

I waited outside for my brother, and as staff members arriving for their shifts saw me, they greeted me warmly, sharing in my joy. When my brother and three friends finally arrived, my happiness knew no bounds. We were in Malmö, and they asked what I wanted to eat. Craving Arabic pastry, we headed to an Arabic restaurant. There, we indulged in delicious pastries, topped with cheese, zaatar, and a medley of other flavours. Each bite was a celebration of my newfound freedom.

(Me and Dyaa outside the prison building)

(Dyaa and I back in Syria)

A Heartfelt Call

At the restaurant, amidst the joy of savouring Arabic pastries, I called my father. His voice on the other end was filled with sheer delight. The sound of his happiness added an extra layer of warmth to my already jubilant day.

Starting Fresh

Later, we bought a mattress, a phone, and other essentials before heading to my brother's house. It felt surreal to be making these ordinary purchases, marking the start of a new chapter in my life. As we settled in, each item symbolised a step towards reclaiming normalcy and building a future beyond the prison walls.

Liberation and Reconnection

That evening, the freedom to do as I pleased was intoxicating. We watched *Shazam*, and I revelled in the luxury of choosing what to watch instead of following a TV guide. Throughout the week, I reconnected with friends. While some kept their distance—an understandable response—others welcomed me back with open arms. As they spent more time with me, they noticed the changes within me, and our bonds grew stronger, enriched by newfound understanding

Betrayed by the Press

A journalist I had met earlier contacted me, and I saw it as an opportunity to show my transformation and regret. He seemed kind and invited me to a restaurant. I shared my story, hoping for a positive article.

But when it was published, it was a disappointment. It painted the same negative picture, briefly mentioning my efforts to change. I felt betrayed and hurt by the hurtful comments that followed.

Rebuilding Hope

I tried to lift my spirits with nature walks and library visits. I even volunteered at the Red Cross in Ängelholm, which felt rewarding. The Kommun helped me financially, allowing me to pay off some debts.

Finding Solace

A few months later, I received news that I no longer needed to report to the police station daily, which was a relief. During this time, I focused on learning new things, improving myself, becoming a game developer, and continually seeking a way to regain my residency.

Confidential Package

Without a residency card, I found myself unable to work, which was a significant setback. The absence of legal status not only hindered my ability to earn a living but also made it challenging to rebuild my life fully. I stayed in close contact with my lawyer, hoping for some form of temporary residency. This would provide me with the opportunity to find employment, secure a stable income, and begin the process of regaining my footing in society. The situation was frustrating and disheartening, but I remained hopeful that a resolution would soon enable me to move forward.

One night, after returning home and checking my email, I discovered a notification that a package from the Migration Office was awaiting pickup. I was filled with anticipation and had to wait until the next day to collect it. As I lay in bed, my mind raced with thoughts of what it might contain, hoping it was my long-awaited residency card.

The morning came, and I hurried to ICA to retrieve the package. It was marked as confidential. With trembling hands, I opened the envelope and peered inside. To my immense joy, it was indeed my residency card! The happiness I felt was beyond words; I was overwhelmed with emotion and tears of joy streamed down my face.

But then... I woke up. The exhilarating moment dissolved into the harsh reality that it had all been a dream. My heart sank as I realised the truth: the package was nothing more than a reply to my lawyer's request, stating the disapproval of my residency application. The crushing disappointment and sadness were almost too much to bear. The dream had painted a vivid picture of hope, only to be replaced by the stark reality of rejection.

Hoping for a Brighter Tomorrow

It's been five long years since I left prison, yet my future remains shrouded in uncertainty. Every day, I yearn for a second chance—to live a decent life, to marry, to have children, and to help others. The dreams of a family and a stable life are what keep me going.

I am pleading with those who hold my fate in their hands to look at my case with compassion and understanding. Living in this constant state of uncertainty is excruciating. I just want the chance to prove that I can be a contributing member of society, that I can love and be loved, that I can give back and make a difference.

My only wish is to live a normal life. I implore you to reconsider my case, to see the person I have become, and to help me find a path out of this limbo. The longing for redemption and the chance to start anew is my deepest desire, and I hope with all my heart that it is within reach.

Adam Youssef

*   *   *

Jag ber Sverige om ursäkt

Your thoughts matter to me.

Please consider rating this book—it would mean a lot.

Social Media

X: *https://x.com/journalvibe*
Facebook: *https://www.facebook.com/profile.php?id=61561039745589*
Instagram: *https://www.instagram.com/thejournalist_10/*
Reddit: *https://www.reddit.com/r/TTM_readers/*
TikTok: *https://www.tiktok.com/@the_journalist_01*
YouTube:
https://www.youtube.com/channel/UC15dw9DuVq1b-DymBgpeWBQ

Contact

Email: *journalvibe@gmail.com*

Copyright Notice

9 798334 227590